Horses & Jumping

Horses & Jumping

Ingvar Fredricson
Anders Gernandt   Gunnar Hedlund
Lars Sederholm

translated by

Captain K. Aschan

advisory editor

Daphne Machin Goodall

Pelham Books

First published in Great Britain by
PELHAM BOOKS LTD
52 Bedford Square
London WC1B 3EF
1976

First published as *Hästar & hoppning*
by J. Beckmans Bokforlag AB, Stockholm, Sweden

ISBN 0 7207 0854 0

Filmset and printed in Great Britain by
BAS Printers Limited, Wallop, Hampshire

Contents

Foreword by Göran Casparsson 7

Introduction by Ingvar Fredricson 9

Nerves — Muscles — Jumping Technique 10

Breeding — Training of Young Horses 34

Select Bibliography 46

Training and Riding Jumping Horses 48

Series of Pictures for the Study of Jumping Techniques 59

- David Broome 60
- Jonqueres d'Oriola 71
- Raimondo d'Inzeo 79
- Harvey Smith 87
- Jan-Olof Wannius 97
- Alwin Schockemöhle 105
- Hans-Günther Winkler 113

The Authors 118

Foreword

During the last few years there has been a tremendous development in all riding activities, so that the need for information and education has increased. This is particularly so in the case of jumping, since the combinations and dimensions of the fences have become increasingly more difficult.

It is for that reason that this book has been produced and it is hoped that riders of show jumpers, trainers and breeders and, of course, all other people who are interested, will find that these observations on the behaviour of the jumping horse are worthwhile. They are based on veterinary scientific investigations — mainly achieved by slow-motion films of horses in action — and give valuable information on what actually happens during approach, jumping and landing. This information should be of value as an addition to earlier observations on the behaviour of horses and riders during these moments. On the basis of veterinary studies, even breeding and education are affected. (When the Swedish Army's need for horse material practically discontinued, it became possible to concentrate on the breeding of thoroughbreds to provide good saddle horses.) It is therefore worthwhile to study the various viewpoints as to how, now more than ever, through breeding one can produce animals with a special ability for jumping. In order to utilize the first years of the horse's life, some interesting, if at times controversial ideas on the education of the foal and the young horse are put forward.

The scientific chapters are completed from the point of view of an experienced trainer regarding the education of riders and horses in the art of jumping.

First class picture material is offered, partly slow-motion photos accompanied by professional comments, partly excellent sketches, which gives the book added delight for all friends of the horse. It will serve as an invaluable foundation for the education of jumping horses.

GÖRAN CASPARSSON
Teacher in jumping, Riding School of Strömsholm

Introduction

From experience we know that some horses have a certain talent for jumping. This talent is due to a natural ability which can be developed through suitable training. Because of this inherited ability, one can say that the horse has a "head for jumping" — or, colloquially, a "jumping head". This indicates, quite rightly, that above all it is the qualities of the horse's central nervous system — the brain and the spinal cord — that are significant. From this, the movements of the horse are controlled. The extent of co-ordination between the central nervous system, the muscles and the organs of sense ultimately decides how good a jumper a horse can become.

How can you produce a good jumping horse? How can you find out if a horse has the qualifications to become a good jumper? How can you effectively develop the qualities that are specially important for jumping? These are questions of interest to most breeders, trainers, riders and veterinary surgeons. Today, we have good veterinary medical basic knowledge of the functions of the horse, together with a lot of practical experience. Against this background we can now go ahead and by thorough research widen our knowledge of the qualities that make up the differences between the jumping horse and others.

Thanks to a new technique — based on slow-motion photography — we can today study the action of jumping horses much more easily. By filming them with up to 500 frames per second we have the opportunity to study objectively and in detail, and to compare different jumping horses. In other words, we have been able to "take apart" the action of the jumping horse, point by point, and then evaluate the importance of the various qualities as a whole.

The purpose of this book is to present, in popular scientific form, some of the conclusions that previous knowledge and this recent research have achieved: the result of conventional breeding principles, objective and effective tests in order to detect the jumping talents of a horse early on and new points of view for the training of jumping horses. With the close co-operation of qualified trainers and riders the description has been completed together with valuable advice and directions.

The book is the result of some stimulating teamwork. I will therefore warmly thank all collaborators for the interest they have shown and the work they have done to make the book as instructive and correct as possible.

Owing to the collaboration of the Army Research Institute in Stockholm and the assistance of Master Engineer Tryggve Ramqvist, suitable photographic equipment was made available and taken to England. I would also like to render my thanks to Captain Nils Ankarcrona, riding instructor Göran Casparsson, Colonel Sven Grape, Captain Olle Kjellander, Professor Sven Landgren, Captain Greger Lewenhaupt, Professor Lennart Nicander, Professor David Ottosson, Mr Sixten Pohl and Surveyor Fredrik Thott for their valuable help.

I would also like to thank Mr Douglas Bunn, ex-Chairman of the British Show Jumping Association, for giving us complete freedom to move about in the jumping arenas and take films during the European Team Competitions at Hickstead.

INGVAR FREDRICSON
Stockholm

Nerves — Muscles — Jumping Technique

A complicated combination of forces

Show jumping of a high international standard makes immense and special demands on the horses competing. Jumping large obstacles is so trying that only a small number of horses have the chance to reach the top. Most of them, even ridden by experienced trainers and riders, will not achieve this.

In order to develop horses suitable for jumping and worth training, the leading riders in Sweden annually study hundreds of competing "possibilities". They look for very special qualities epitomized in a phrase, the so called "jumping head". One knows that above all it is the qualities in the horse's central nervous system — brain and spinal cord — that decide how good a jumper a horse can be. The horses may be of various types, but they all have this quality in common, which makes for an outstanding talent for jumping. At the Veterinary High School in Stockholm, research into the jumping horse's various movements is at present in progress. Against a background of basic veterinary medical knowledge with the aid of advanced techniques — amongst other things slow-motion photography — this research gives additional possibilities of study and appreciation of the various qualities that are important for a good jumping horse.

The function and co-ordination of the central nervous system, the muscles and the organs of sense are decisive for the horse's balance, canter action, judgement of distance, ability to jump, etc. The knowledge of these functions is, in other words, essential for the correct judgement of a future jumping horse. We want to present here a readily comprehensive scientific description of the functions of the central nervous system, the muscles and the organs of sense. This is the background to fairly new and well thought out principles for future ability tests, breeding and training of jumping horses in Sweden.

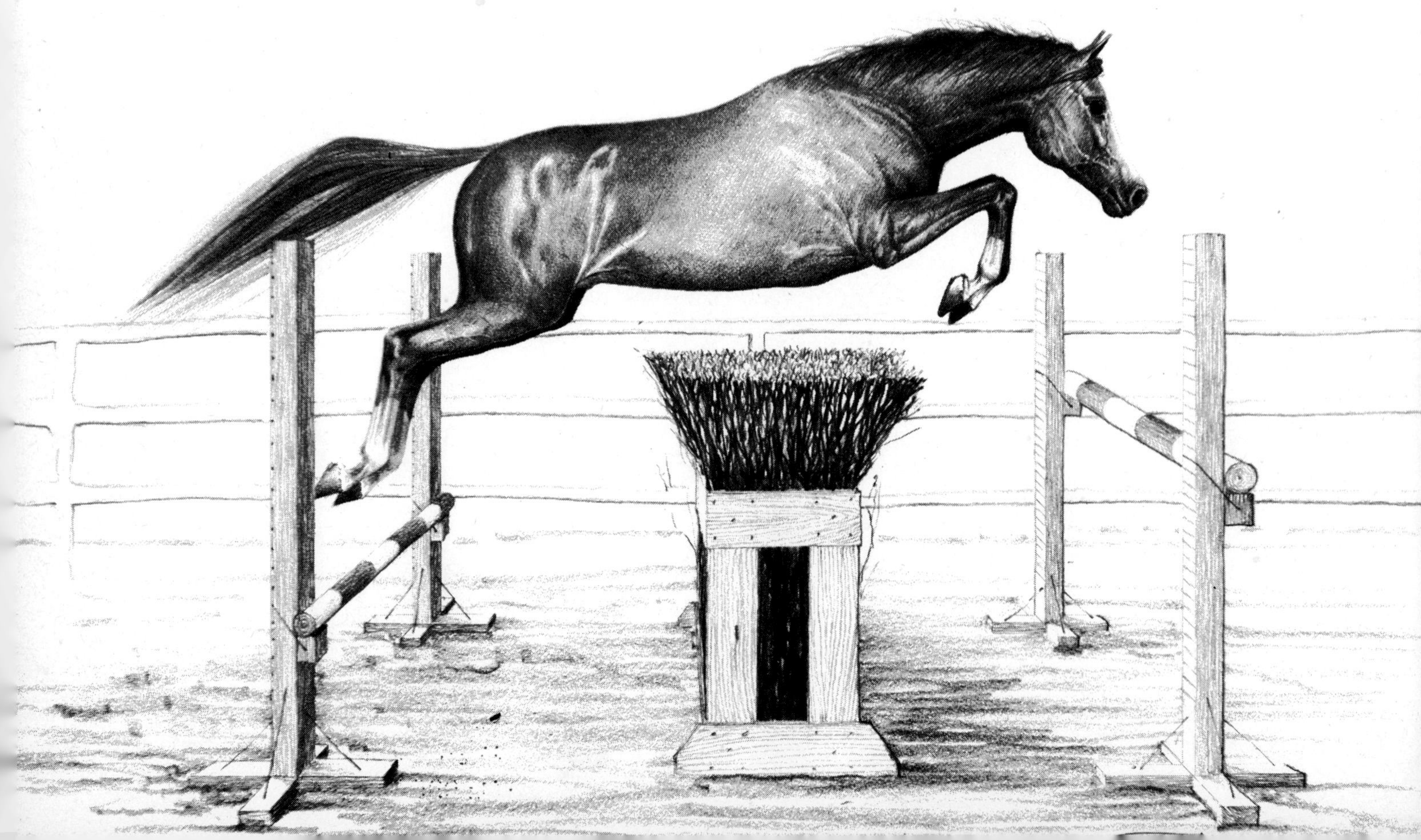

The brain

The brain of a horse, as in all other mammals, could, up to a point, be compared with a computer. A computer is constructed in such a way that with certain given prerequisites it is able to execute various tasks. In order to exploit the possibilities of a computer, one must first "teach" it certain programmes. If you then give it the necessary information, it can follow its programmed instructions and answer with a result — an addition, a conclusion, etc.

We assume that the brain is the horse's own computer and able to assimilate data. In the same way he must learn to make use of his talents and must be stimulated with correct information. The original built-in possibilities for the brain to execute different operations are inherited by the horse. One assumes, for instance, that in the central nervous system (CNS) there are inherited patterns for different paces. One could say that these patterns correspond with data programmes which, however, have no definite formation, but could always be modified.

Early programming

The data programmes for the horse's various movements develop during the early foetus stage. Owing to a ripening process of the nervous system and the movement apparatus, the foetus soon begins to make various movements. The development now proceeds gradually during the whole period of gestation, and the movements of the foal are relatively well developed at birth.

While the horse is growing, constant modifications of the inherited data programmes occur as the growth of the skeleton, muscles and joints changes the body's proportions and, consequently, movement conditions. The experiences which the foal and the young horse acquire during play and other activities have a decisive impact on the ripening process that continues within the CNS. The precision and effectiveness in the movements of the foal gradually increase.

The movements of the grown horse that we observe are, in other words, the result partly of inherited programmes and potential within the CNS, partly of modifications of these programmes by external influences (new information received by the brain) brought about by balance, eyesight, hearing and other impressions of the senses.

For example: when a horse is cantering towards a high fence, the CNS continuously sends nerve impulses to various muscle groups. Well adjusted co-ordination by these muscles produces the joint movements that build up the typical pattern for canter action.

The action must enable the horse to take the fence but, at the same time, the CNS must receive further information of the body's relation to the outside world. As we said, this information comes from the various senses — eyesight, hearing, balance, etc. When the external conditions are changed, the CNS is able, thanks to the information received by the senses, to modify the flow of impulse. In this manner the canter action is continually adjusted to the external demands.

For example, if a rider wants to alter the jumping technique of his horse, he must influence the CNS through his aids and training methods. In this way he controls the complicated co-ordination between the CNS, the different senses and the muscles which in detail decides all the horse's movements.

Training improves the brain "programming"

By correct systematic schooling the inherited programmes can be adjusted to enable the horse to cope with special activities — such as show jumping.

Training improves the horse's mental reactions, and impulses from the nervous system to the muscles are effectively co-ordinated. Incorrect training obviously works the other way, and promising young horses may be totally ruined.

In this respect it is the youngster who is most affected. In Sweden we believe that the earlier one can begin training a particular movement, the better the results. It is well known that the more often a special movement can be repeated, the sooner and more correctly it will be performed. Without repetition one learns nothing. This fact is the basis of all schooling and training exercises for horses and humans alike.

Muscles — red and white

A muscle is composed of a great mass of threads of which there are two types:

a) the red muscle fibres which are strong but contract slowly.

b) the white muscle fibres which contract faster but are less tough.

The relation between the red and white fibres in a muscle is inherited and varies in both breeds and individuals. The Thoroughbred — with its fast action — naturally has more white fibres in a muscle than a cart horse. Such variation is notable in different jumping horses which have similar conformation.

This is interesting, as the greatest fence height a horse can negotiate depends on the speed with which the joints of the extremities can stretch during the take-off. It is necessary that the jumping horse should be full of impulsion in his jumping action. It must be remembered that certain half-bred horses also have the same distribution of red and white fibres and that their muscles are able to contract with astounding speed.

Impulsion

In order to obtain the highest possible impulsion in the take-off a great number of red and white fibres must function simultaneously. Further, these fibres must have such training that they produce great power when contracted. Through suitable training the cross-section face of the muscles (and thereby power) can be increased, which is the condition for the horse's ability to collect himself during the approach and maximum impulsion in the take-off. Without a sufficient number of white fibres in the muscles of his extremities a horse, however well trained, will never become a successful jumper.

Muscle co-ordination

Muscle co-ordination is decisive for the speed and precision of the movements. Examination of top athletes shows that their muscle co-ordination is quite different from that of untrained people. Owing to inherited ability and training the successful human high jumper has a special ability to co-ordinate different muscle groups and, during certain movements, to use muscle groups that are not used by untrained people. Clearly this is also the case with the best jumping horses.

One-sidedness

Like many other animal species the horse has certain differences in his co-ordinating ability in the near and off-sides of his body. This laterality is called stiffness by many riders, although one-sidedness is a better word. Most horses are considered to be stiff to the left which means that they seek more support from the left rein. This stiffness is recognized by dressage trainers whose main objective, of course, is to "straighten" the horse.

With suitable training the horse should be encouraged to seek equal support from both reins and use both hindlegs to the same extent. The fundamental principle is to train the muscles of the "soft side", i.e. the right side of a horse obliquely to the left. To make this a success, the rider should consistently work on the horse's CNS in such a manner that the difference in the muscle co-ordination is eliminated. Because most riders themselves have lateral problems, only very few are able successfully to straighten their horses.

The horse's senses

A rider can never fully understand how his horse copes with the world around him. This lack of communication often causes problems. Some riders will even try to fight against the natural behaviour of the horse, forgetting that it was established millions of years ago. It goes without saying that this will not improve relations between horse and rider.

When the rider eventually finds that he cannot achieve what he seeks to attain, it is all too easy to blame the horse for this failure. He doesn't realize the difficulties that are caused because he has put his own interpretation on the horse's reaction to outside influences. Knowledge of the structure and function of the different organs of sense is therefore of great significance when it comes to avoiding the wrong interpretation of the horse's behaviour. It is essential to understand this to enable the training to develop naturally, without arresting the horse's inherited ability.

The eyesight

The eyesight of different animal species has, to a great extent, been determined by the circumstances in which a given species has developed. It is therefore impossible to make comparisons between, for example, the eyesight of man and horse. Unfortunately, the vision of the horse is not fully known, but as it is of great importance for show jumping, we will try to explain how the horse *probably* sees the outside world.

Also, the CNS interpretation of the different signals from the eye may be improved by systematic training. It is therefore possible to adapt the horse's vision for show jumping more successfully than has been possible to date.

Irregular curve and immobile lens

There are two fundamental differences in the construction of the human eye and that of the horse. The retina — the part of the eye that translates the picture to nerve impulses — of the horse's eye has an irregular curve. One also assumes that the horse doesn't change the shape of the lens in order to focus the picture. This means that in order to focus the picture, the horse must either raise or lower his eye. To attain this, he takes a rough aim by altering the position of the head and then perfects it with the aid of small eye movements.

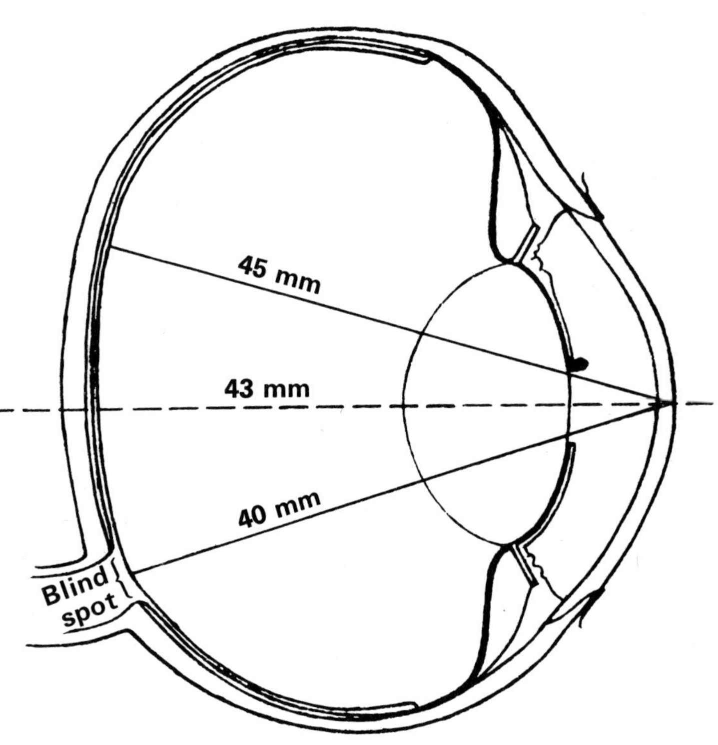

Figure 1. The back part of the horse's eye is not symmetrical. The distance from the optic nerve to the retina varies. As distinguished from the human eye, the horse's eye's adjustment to distance is effected by elevating or lowering the gaze, not by the lens altering its shape.

Figure 2. The horse's field of vision. The horse sees the outer world with both eyes at once or with only one eye. The squared patch can be seen with both eyes simultaneously (60 degrees), the lined area with one eye and the black field not at all.

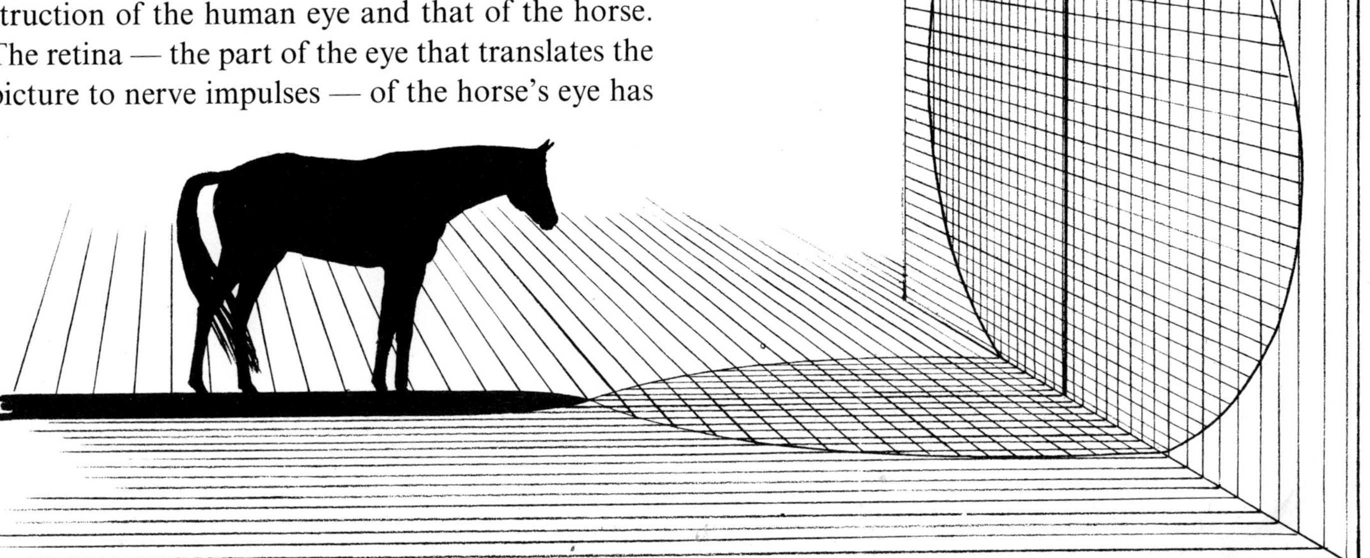

The range of vision is narrow

The total range of vision is the area which the horse can see with both eyes simultaneously and with each eye separately. If the horse looks at an object with both eyes simultaneously, he receives better information than if he uses one eye only. Thus one often observes a horse turning his head in order to focus an object with both eyes.

The size of the vision area is of particular importance for the horse's ability to judge a fence. The shape of his nose bridge and the position of his eyes influence the extent of this common field of vision. Thus a Roman nose and widely spaced eyes will improve his chances of being able to see an object with both eyes simultaneously. (See Figure 4).

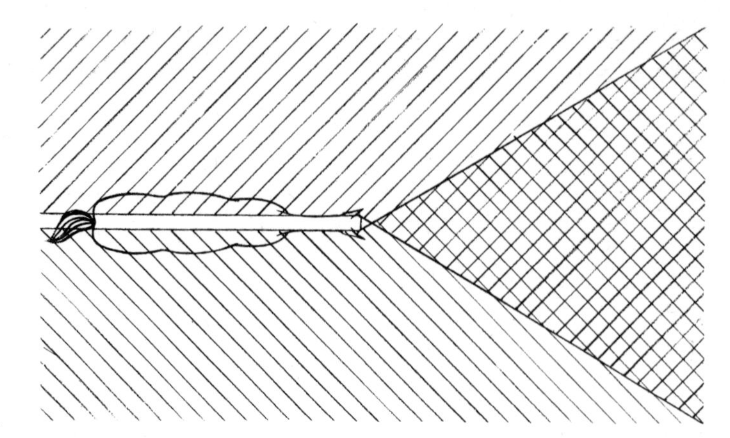

Figure 3. The horse's field of vision. With his head elevated and pointed straight forward the horse will see the squared patch with both eyes, the lined area with one eye only, and the white strip not at all.

For a horse to judge a fence accurately, it is not enough for him to be able to see it with both eyes simultaneously — he must see it sharply outlined. To get the upper parts of a fence sharply outlined, the horse must gradually elevate his gaze as he gets closer to the fence. This means that he will see less of the fence with both eyes simultaneously. During the act of jumping, he can see nothing of the fence with both eyes simultaneously, nor can he see the part of the fence under the front feet or body. Thus when the horse has made the take-off jump, he cannot, with the aid of his eyesight, judge how high he must bend his front legs to avoid knocking down the fence.

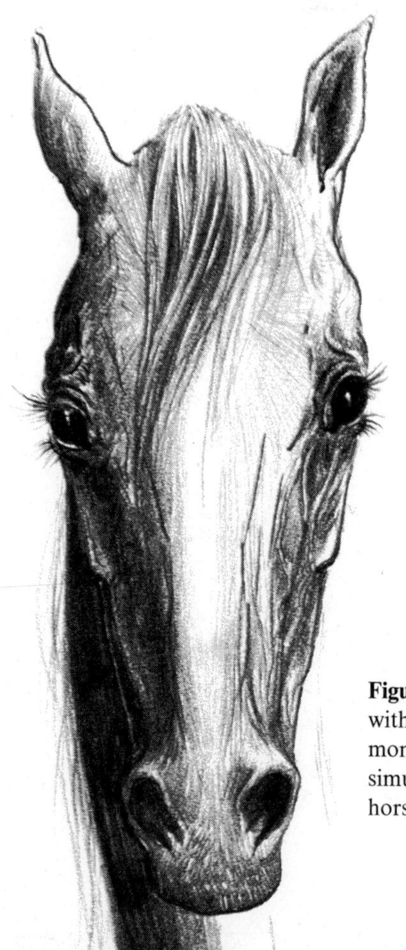

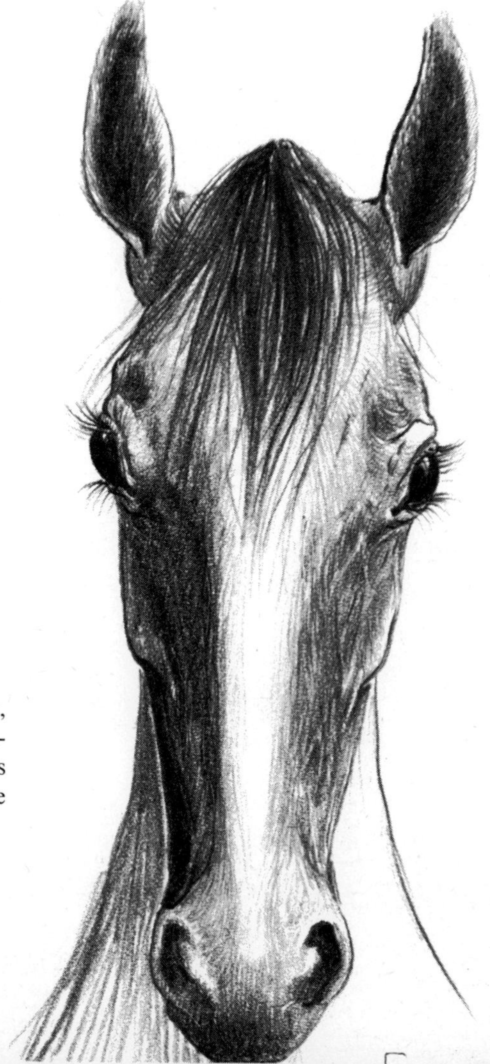

Figure 4. For the horse on the right, with eyes placed to the side, the common field of vision for both eyes simultaneously is less than for the horse on the left.

The horse lacks our dimensional range of vision

The horse's judgement of distance is complicated and is based on several different factors. Most likely the horse lacks the far-sighted vision of man. Theoretically, one must presume that the horse's judgement of distance is inferior to man's — especially at close range. This has also been proved in practice.

The most important mechanism for the horse's judgement of distance is the so-called parallax. In ophthalmology — the science of the eye — the parallax signifies the change of the optical angle between different objects which follows when the body or the head is moved. A close object seems to move more than one that is further away.

During normal breeding conditions, the foal and the young horse move about mostly on relatively even ground. They therefore learn mainly to co-ordinate and use their various mechanisms to solve the problem of distance and to judge the position of objects on the ground.

When later on the horse, during training, has to learn to judge the distance of a barrier above the ground surface, a new and unfamiliar situation is created. The co-ordination between the mechanisms for his ability to judge distance is broken. (See Figure 7.) There is no doubt that many of the problems which occur in connection with the jumping training of an inexperienced 4-year-old are due to this confusion in his judgement of distance. If, on the other hand, one starts early on to accustom the horse to judge the distance to objects of different heights, he will more effectively learn how to use the mechanisms most suitable for jumping. Many of the problems can thus be avoided.

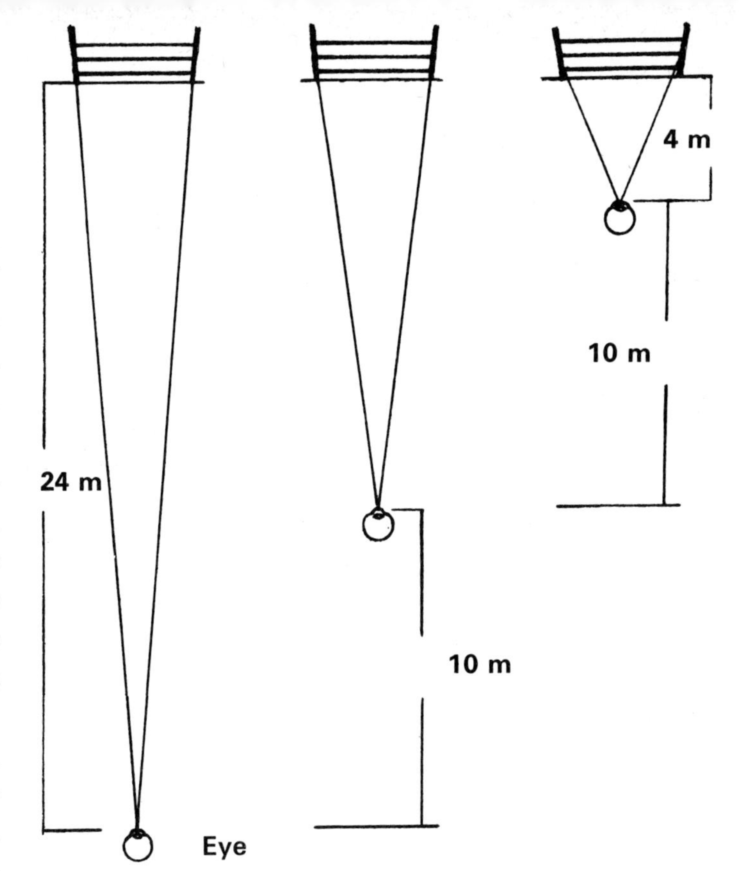

Figure 5. Judgement of distance through parallax. The width of the fence seems to increase faster, the closer the horse gets. From the left to the middle sketch the distance differs by 10 m and the angle by 5 degrees. Between the middle and the right sketch the distance also differs by 10 m but the angle by 30 degrees.

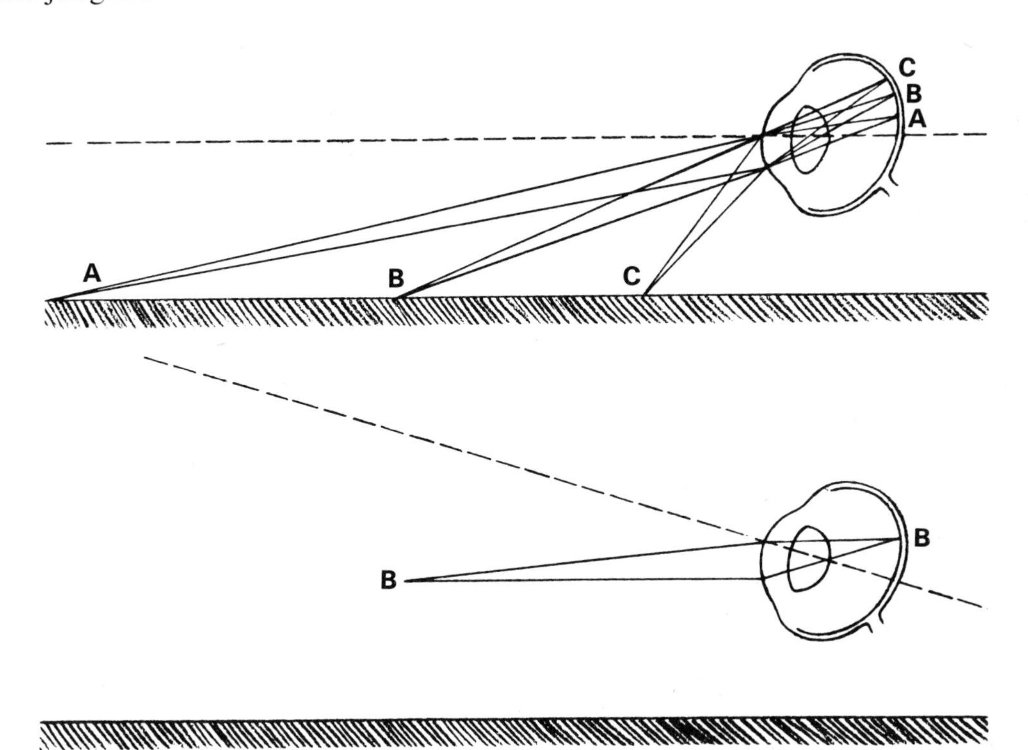

Figure 6. When a horse looks at a distant object on the ground (A), the light rays must break on a certain spot on the retina (A) to make the object sharp. The nearer the object gets (C) the higher up on the retina the picture must fall to make the horse see the object clearly (C). The dotted line is the optic angle of the eye.

Figure 7. In order to focus on close objects above ground level the horse must elevate his gaze. The dotted line is the optic angle of the eye.

Figure 8:1. The horse elevates his head and neck simultaneously as soon as his forelegs have left the ground. Thus the forelegs stretch and the hindlegs bend by reflex.

Figure 8:2. Immediately before the landing, head and neck are elevated, whereby the same reflex is released as at the take-off with the forelegs.

upwards, downwards and to either side. The small sense cells and nerves in the joints, muscles and sinews release nerve impulses to various parts of the CNS with the result that different groups of muscles in the extremities are activated.

1. When the neck is raised, the hindlegs bend and the forelegs stretch. The effect of this reflex shows interesting similarities with the horse's behaviour during the first phase of the take-off and in connection with the landing. (See Figures 8:1 and 8:2.)

2. When the neck is bent downwards, the hindlegs stretch while the frontlegs bend. This movement is similar to the second phase of the take-off. At the same time, the horse stretches his neck forwards-downwards, the hindlegs stretch powerfully during take-off while the forelegs bend so as not to hit the fence. (See Figure 9.)

3. When the neck is bent or turned to one side, the foreleg and hindleg of the same side are stretched. This reflex is used when the horse is taking a sharp turn. (See Figure 10.)

Balance reflexes

Besides the reflexes already mentioned which aim to keep the head in a normal position, the sense of balance even releases reflexes with the same effect as the neck reflexes of types 1 and 2 (see above):

Figure 9. During the second phase of the take-off, the neck is stretched and bent downwards, releasing reflexes that bend the forelegs and stretch the hindlegs.

Figure 10. A change of direction at high speed. The horse turns head and neck in the opposite direction, thereby releasing reflexes that counteract the centrifugal force.

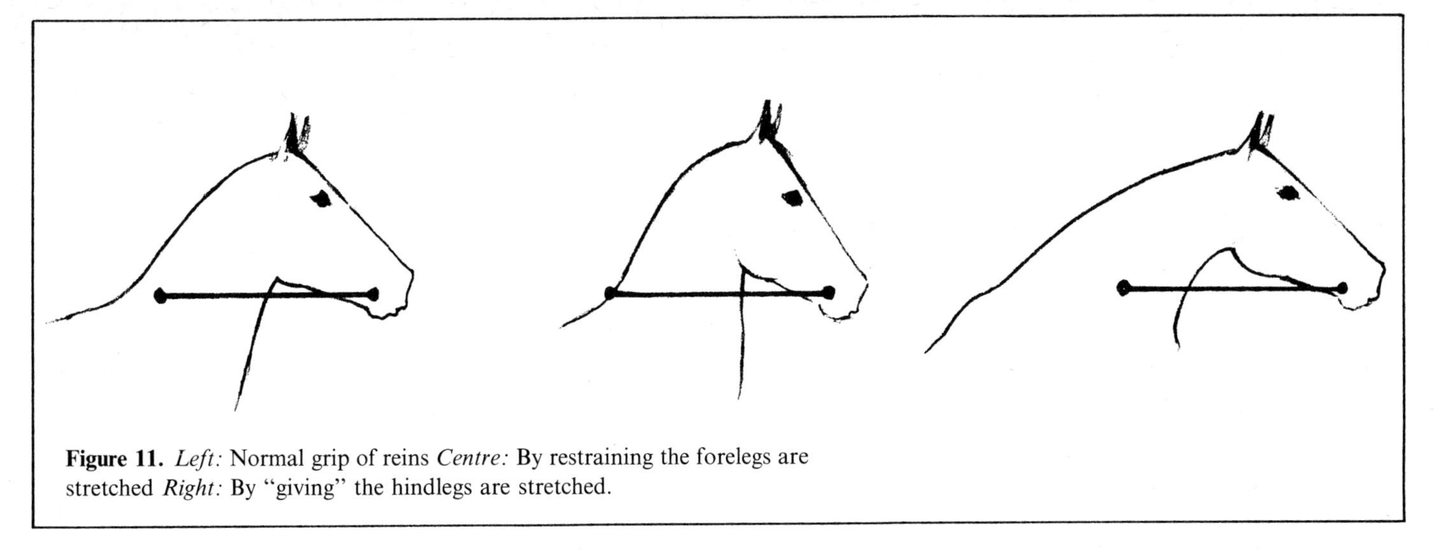

Figure 11. *Left:* Normal grip of reins *Centre:* By restraining the forelegs are stretched *Right:* By "giving" the hindlegs are stretched.

i) When the head is held vertically, the forelegs stretch and the hindlegs bend.
(ii) If the head is held horizontally, the forelegs bend and the hindlegs stretch.
A rider with a fine sense of touch may utilize these reflexes. The effects of certain aids with the reins, which includes "feeling" the horse's mouth — or "feeling with the reins" — are best explained in the following manner. The purpose of these aids is to get a more powerful take-off with the forelegs and more impulsion with the hindlegs. To obtain this result, it is necessary to apply the aids at exactly the right moment. (See Figure 11.)

The effect of the reins in connection with "feeling"
The "feeling" aid consists of two phases — one restraining (holding back) and one "giving" (releasing). The restraining "feel" must be applied so that the neck and balance of type 1 co-ordinate. Also, the restraining "feel" must come when, during the first phase of the take-off, the forelegs have touched the ground and take-off is imminent. If restraint on the reins is applied too early or too late, it will either lose effect or the horse will be disturbed.
The "give" should be applied to cause the neck and balance type 2 to co-ordinate. The "give" must be offered as the horse begins the take-off with the hindlegs during the second phase of the take-off. As "feeling" demands extreme sense of rhythm in the rider, it should not be recommended to inexperienced riders.
The neck reflex of type 3 should be used by all riders. Everybody knows how difficult it can be to negotiate a sharp turn on a slippery track. If the rider turns his horse in the opposite direction to the one in which he is going, the outer pair of legs will stretch. The horse is thus given greater opportunities to counteract the influence of the centrifugal force. When moving freely, the horse uses the very same reflex himself.

Causes of disturbances

Through the information provided by the sense faculties the CNS is given opportunities to judge distance, speed, acceleration, etc. In this way the nerve impulses that go to the muscles can always be adapted to the many different demands which are forced upon the horse by his environment. The competing horse, for example, has to overcome a great number of external and internal disturbances.

Pains
Pains in the extremities and the back are common causes of disturbance. The sensation of pain affects the CNS and the impulse wave is changed in order to save the area under stress as much as possible. Thus other parts of the movement apparatus will act as substitutes — and the horse may become lame.

The ground foundation
Another important cause of disturbance, which very often goes unheeded, is that the jumping horse has to compete on different types of ground. This greatly affects the jumping ability and

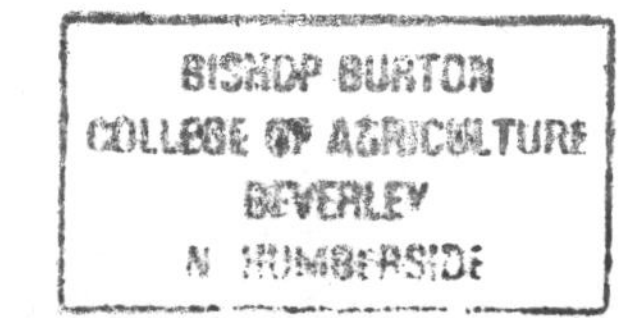

Figure 12.

Figure 13.

soundness of the horse. To canter one day on a springy turf track and another on a hard, "dead" sand track demands much of the horse's adaptability. The change from one track to another is often expressed by stiffening of the muscles, soreness and tiredness. Also, a change of weather may cause difficulties. A wet slippery track puts a great deal of strain on the horse, as the co-ordination of his muscles must be varied considerably.

Care of feet and shoeing

One cause of disturbance that should not be allowed to occur is faultiness in the care of the feet and shoeing. It is amazing how many competition riders seem to lack a feeling of responsibility regarding the correct shoeing of their horses. It often happens unnecessarily that even successful and valuable horses have to take part in a difficult competition while incorrectly shod.

The rider

In this connection, we must not forget the rider who — with his weight alone — subjects the horse to obvious disturbances. Besides, it is difficult for the rider to adjust his point of gravity correctly in all situations to that of the horse.

Jumping technique

When a horse is going to jump a fence, the action can be divided into different stages:

☐ The canter action during the approach.
☐ The first part of the take-off.
☐ The second part of the take-off.
☐ The parabola above the fence.
☐ The landing.
☐ The first stride after landing.

Canter

The action can be divided into two main parts:
1) Support when the horse has one or more feet on the ground.
2) And when all four feet are off the ground.

Three-time canter
The normal tempo of the canter is a three-time and this means that the feet touch the ground on three separate moments. The canter to the left is characterized by the horse making the following movements: 1) at the canter the horse lands on his off hindfoot, 2) at the same time applies the near hindfoot and off forefoot and 3) puts down the near forefoot. (See Figures 12 and 13.) The near foreleg is called the leading leg and gives this canter its name — left canter. The horse has, during this type of canter, one, two or three legs in contact with the ground. When the leading foreleg leaves the ground, the support is withdrawn and momentarily all four feet leave the ground, to be terminated when the off hindfoot touches the ground.

Figure 14.

Collection

Through training, the horse can be made to increase the impulsion of the hindlegs, whereby his centre of gravity is projected closer to the point of application by the hindlegs. Thus, the hindlegs will carry more of the horse's weight — the horse canters with increased collection. This displacement of the point of gravity is important for the take-off. When collection is increased, the simultaneous application of the diagonal pair of feet is lost — the canter becomes a four-time one. (See Figure 14.)

In a four-time canter to the left, the feet are used in the following order:

1. Off hindfoot. 2. Near hindfoot. 3. Off forefoot. 4. The leading near forefoot.

By studying the pictures further on, you will find that this is the type of collection that the competing riders strive to attain when approaching the various fences. This is natural, as the four-time canter offers opportunities for a more concentrated collection than the three-time canter.

On the forehand

Sometimes the application of the diagonals can be reversed — i.e. the foreleg is used before the diagonal hindleg. A horse cantering in this way goes "on his forehand", as it were, and the order in a canter to the right is as follows:

1. Near hindfoot. 2. Near forefoot. 3. Off hindfoot. 4. The leading right foreleg. (See Figure 15.)

If a horse is "going on his forehand", you will see

Figure 15.

the experienced rider strive to get the horse's centre of gravity projected backwards. This is often the condition for clearing the fence.
While approaching a fence, it is of great importance to be able to maintain a correct collected balance, even if the tempo is increased. If the rhythm or tempo is too slow, the horse loses impulsion. If the tempo is increased, many horses may lose their collection and thus get on the forehand.

Fast gallop
At further increased tempo, the canter successively becomes a typical gallop. In a gallop to the right, the order of application is as follows:
1. Near hindfoot. 2. Off hindfoot. 3. Near forefoot. 4. The leading off foreleg. (See Figure 16.) Because of the high speed, the horse will have only one or two feet simultaneously in contact with the ground. The time during which all four feet leave the ground will increase, the faster the horse gallops.

The first part of the take-off

The last stride of the approach has a different character to the others and should really be called the first stride of the take-off. Usually the horse has increased the impulsion of the hindlegs and thereby the collection. The hindfeet are put down at a certain distance from one another, which may

Figure 16.

Figure 17.

vary from leap to leap; one finds, when jumping on a sand track, that the feet have slid and this is an indication that the horse has braked. (See Figures 17, 18, 19.)

The forehand is lowered as the forelegs reach further forwards than normally, during the final seconds of the take-off. Because of this, the horse is able to obtain greater impulsion from the fore-hand, partly through muscle activity which strengthens the joints of the extremities, and partly

Figure 18.

through a passive lifting of the quarters. The hindlegs have left the ground just before the elevation of the forelegs begins. The elevation is facilitated when the horse is fully collected and therefore projects his body towards the fence. It is important for the second part of the take-off that the action of the hindlegs occurs immediately after the forefeet have left the ground. During the second phase of the take-off the hindlegs can thus be suitably placed in relation to the horse's centre of

Figure 19.

Figure 20.

gravity in order to obtain a proper elevation. To avoid counteracting this, during the first part of the elevation the rider should not lean forwards too early. The hindfeet are often put on the ground somewhat closer than in a normal jump. But one notices variations on how the approach suits the horse.

The second part of the take-off

When the forehand begins the elevation and before the hindfeet touch the ground there is a short moment when all four feet have left the ground, and now the second part of the take-off begins. This lasts until the hindlegs again leave the ground. To facilitate the displacement of the centre of gravity, head and neck are elevated. (See Figures 20, 21, 22, 23, 24.) The hindfeet are often put down close together in order to get simultaneous and concentrated impulsion. If the horse gets too near the fence, the hindfeet act momentarily as a brake. In a really good take-off, on the other hand, the hindfeet are put down further apart.

When the hindfeet touch the ground, the joints

Figure 22.

Figure 23.

Figure 21.

are straightened and then bent in order to obtain the greatest possible impulsion which gives the horse the forwards-upwards movement over the fence. This effort of stretching is full of impulsion and is terminated only when the feet leave the ground.

The parabola over the fence

During the second phase of the take-off the horse begins to bend the forelegs in order not to knock down the fence. The legs remain bent until the fence is cleared and then he prepares for a landing by again stretching his forelegs.

The hindlegs bend when they leave the ground. Different horses use different methods to prevent the hindlegs from knocking down the fence. Usually, the legs remain bent until the fence is cleared, but some horses, for example, kick out behind at this tricky moment. When the fence has been cleared, the horse will try very quickly to bring his hindlegs forwards-downwards and thus prepare for the landing. If you study the pictures further on, you will see clearly that the ability of different horses to arch their backs varies considerably.

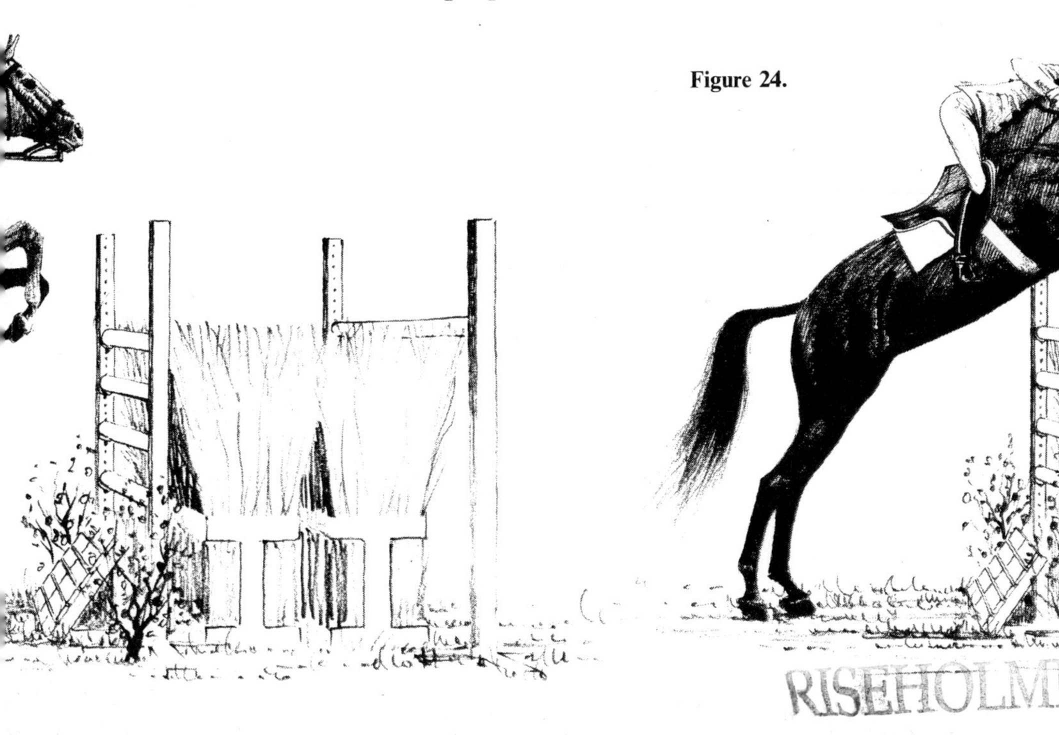
Figure 24.

Figure 25.

The landing

When the fence has been negotiated, the forelegs are stretched and the feet are more or less close together. Immediately before the landing they open in such a manner that first one, then the other touches the ground, in order to take the weight independently. This technique is necessary because of the horse's anatomical construction, so designed that he cannot bend a burdened foreleg. This mechanism, however, involves a risk of the horse stumbling if he happens to land with both forelegs simultaneously. (See Figure 25.)

The first stride after the landing

On landing, the horse's impulsion is directed forwards-downwards and as the forefeet are put down, this must be conveyed forwards. The equilibrium is thus lost and, to regain it, the horse must make a long and quick stride.

The rider is also affected by the change of direction of impulsion.

His body is thrown forwards and he must counteract this. If not, the horse's problem of balance will be further aggravated and he must increase the length of his stride after landing. This is of great importance, especially with close fence combinations.

Immediately after, or at the same time the front feet are elevated to make the first stride after the landing, the hindfeet are put down. The action of the hindlegs then co-operates, enabling the forelegs to find a suitable place so that the horse can regain his balance and thus resume a normal canter action.

The actual parabola

The curve described by the centre of gravity of both horse and rider is similar to a parabola. The form of the curve depends on three factors:

☐ The speed of the approach.
☐ The angle of elevation. (See Figure 26.)
☐ Impulsion.

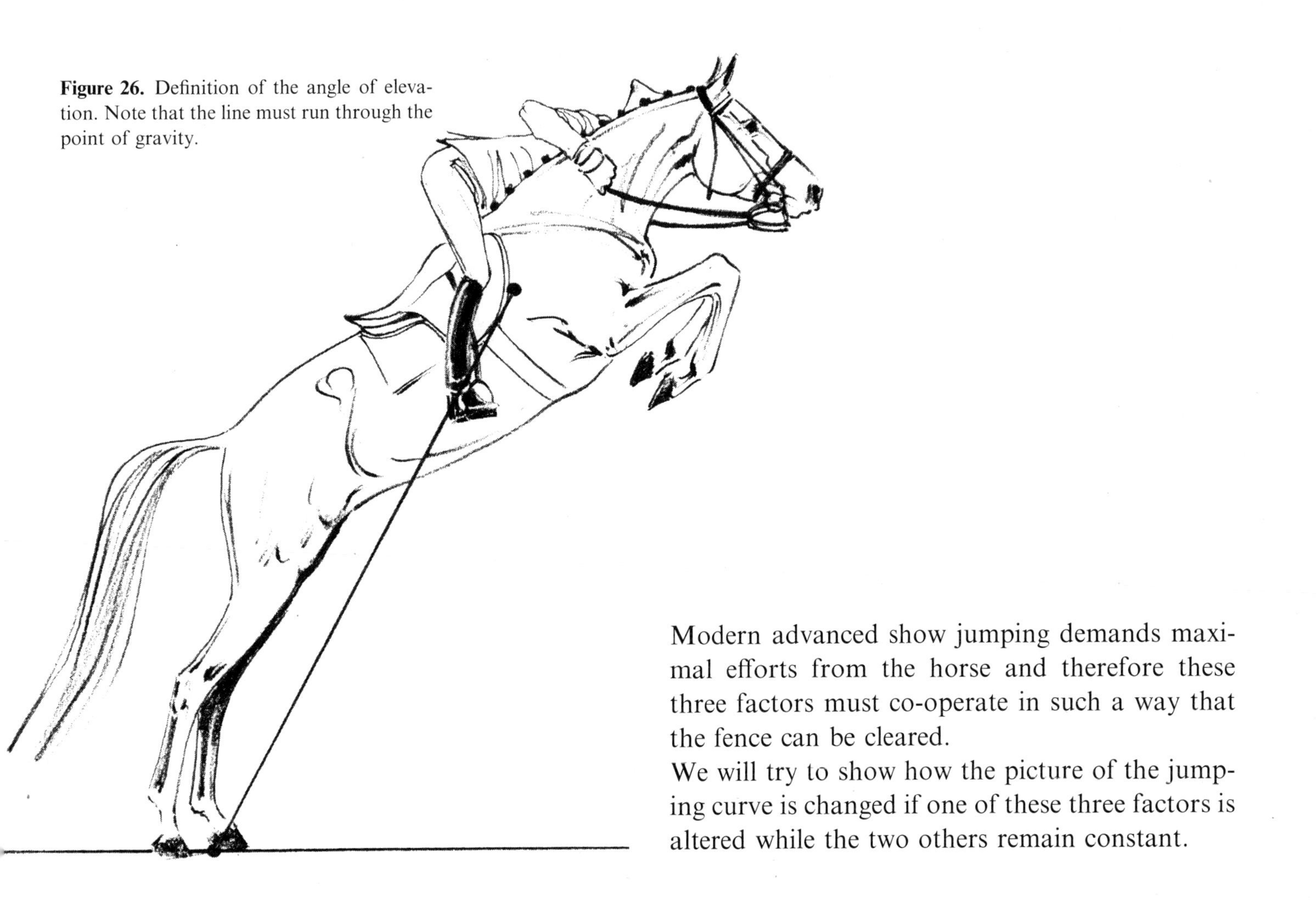

Figure 26. Definition of the angle of elevation. Note that the line must run through the point of gravity.

Modern advanced show jumping demands maximal efforts from the horse and therefore these three factors must co-operate in such a way that the fence can be cleared.
We will try to show how the picture of the jumping curve is changed if one of these three factors is altered while the two others remain constant.

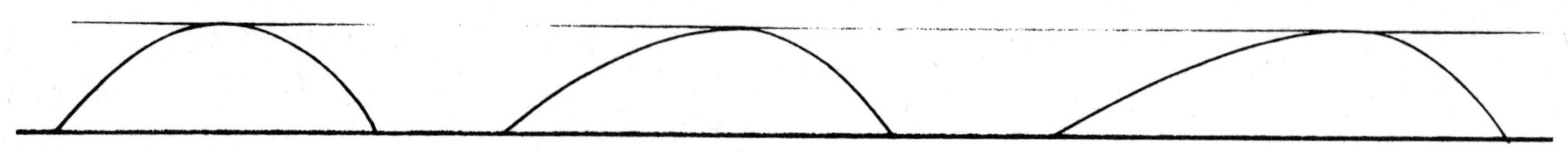

Figure 27. The influence of speed on the curve of the leap. On the left, the speed is low and the leap short. When speed is increased during the approach, the curve becomes longer. Note that the height of the curve of the leap remains unaltered.

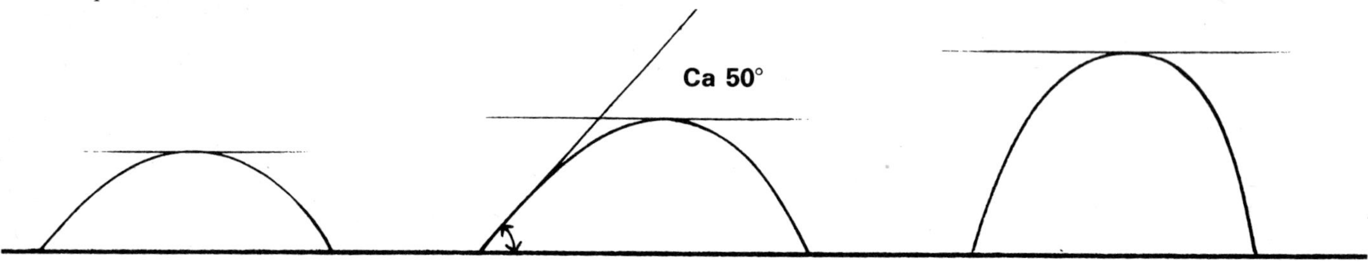

Figure 28. The effect of the angle of elevation on the curve of the leap. The leap reaches its maximum length when the angle is about 50 degrees. A smaller or longer angle makes the leap shorter.

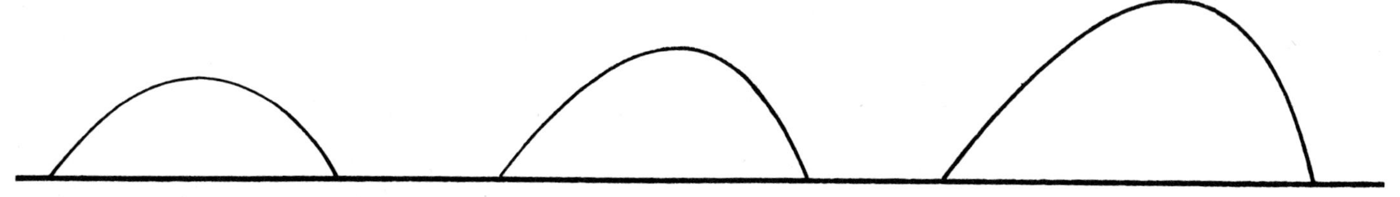

Figure 29. The influence of impulsion on the curve of the leap. If the impulsion from the hindlegs is increased, the leap is increased both in length and height.

The speed of approach varies
The faster the speed of approach, the longer the leap. Note that the height remains unaltered. (See Figure 27.)

The angle of elevation varies
The wider the angle, the higher the leap. The greatest height is achieved at 50 degrees. (See Figure 28.)

Impulsion varies
The greater the impulsion from the hindlegs, the higher and longer the leap. (See Figure 29.)

Jumping over different fences

When the horse jumps a straight up-and-down fence, the experienced rider can vary the pace of the take-off within a relatively wide area. The higher the fence, the narrower the area and the greater the demand for precision in the approach and take-off. The greater the efficiency of the horse, the greater are the possibilities of varying the line of take-off.

An experienced horse, badly ridden, may lose against a mediocre horse handled by a clever rider. How the rider should act in order to make the most of his horse's ability is something for the experts to decide. We can only furnish advice based on what has been recorded earlier.

Fifty degrees for height and length
The elevation ability is important for many reasons. When a horse takes off too near the fence, he must be able to lift himself very quickly to avoid knocking it down.

The Artillery know that cannon must be pointed at a fifty degree angle to make the projectile travel as far as possible. The same applies to several kinds of athletics (e.g. discus throwing) and horse jumping. In other words, it is possible to vary the length and height of a leap by varying the angle of elevation. The impression of the size and thickness of the fence — the degree of compactness — is important for the horse's will to lift himself over. A wall or compact oxer gives an impression of great thickness, while a water jump, on the whole, doesn't give any impression of density at all.

Height without length

The height of a fence is the only factor that decides the elevation curve over a straight up-and-down fence without width. With a suitable combination of approach, speed and elevation the line of take-off can be varied without the horse using more impulsion. Compared with a wall, a fragile combination gives a poor impression of density. When approaching it the rider must therefore pay attention to collecting his horse in order to avoid the curve of the elevation being too low.

Height and length

An oxer is a combination of height and width. As distinguished from the shape of a straight up-and-down fence, the elevation curve over an oxer is determined by two factors. The horse must jump both high and far. Principally the same condition applies to triple bars. The difference in height between the front and rear parts of the fence allows the horse to choose the take-off point closer to the fence without fear of knocking down the front part. With the front and rear bars at the same height and the distance between them increased, the fence becomes more difficult to jump. This can be done without exceeding the accepted maximum measurements for that particular class of competition. The difficulty is that the line of take-off must be chosen with accuracy.

High and wide

For a leap over a high and wide fence there is always a certain angle of elevation that is most suitable. For a parallel oxer, for example, the most suitable angle is slightly longer than 50 degrees. In other words, to obtain this angle, one must choose the correct line of take-off. Thus, with the least possible effort, the horse will avoid knocking down any of the bars. If the angle of elevation is increased, the rear bar will be knocked down; if it is reduced, the front bar will fall.
While jumping combinations, one must notice the difference of the possible variations between an oxer and a straight up-and-down fence. The possibilities of varying the parabola over the first obstacle are greater at an oxer than a straight up-and-down fence. This is important when clearing an exaggerated distance.

Water jumps

When one considers that the length of a leap over an oxer sometimes exceeds 10 m, it is surprising that a water jump of only 5 m can create problems. If these occur, it is obvious that the rider does not know how to utilize the horse's ability to jump water. The difficulty is to make the horse lift himself sufficiently. A rider who can make his horse lift to about 50 degrees should have no difficulty in clearing a water jump, even if the take-off is 1—2 m too soon.

A short stride is good . . .

A horse with a relatively short and energetic stride has the greatest natural qualifications for adjusting his stride to make the distance between two fences come just right. Necessary corrections can be made when taking further strides. The less he has to modify his stride, the easier it is for a horse to retain his balance.

. . . and long strides are shortened

With suitable training, a long-striding horse can be made to vary the length of his stride. The shortening of the stride is achieved mainly through increased collection, whereby an even greater ability to lift himself is obtained.
An untrained horse will try to make the correction on the approach to the take-off. This is not, of course, very effective. One of the rider's first tasks is to correct the length of his horse's strides in time.

We analyse in order to construct

Show jumping in an arena is difficult. It is therefore important to discover early on the horse's talent for jumping, to find out the necessary qualities and learn how to improve the ability to jump.

Top trainers and top riders know intuitively from experience and from the long hours of schooling "how to do it". They also know that a good jumper will be successful if trained correctly and aided by a good rider. However, if a horse lacks a "jumping head", training is wasted.

If we penetrate deeper into the problem, we find that intuition is not sufficient. One must find a sounder basis from which to judge how best to combine all the qualities that are necessary in a good show jumper. How to improve breeding, how to discover in a yearling a natural turn for jumping and how best to pursue the training etc.

We believe that one must very carefully consider and analyse the different qualities that make a good jumping horse. In Sweden our way of analysing the action of jumping is only one of many, and is still open to improvement. It has, however, the advantage of giving the reader opportunities to reach practical conclusions — about breeding, testing natural abilities, training of young horses. Our own practical results will be presented in the next section.

Breeding — Training of Young Horses

Towards better results in competitions

Everybody engaged in breeding half-breds aims to produce better horses. This is quite natural — for otherwise the work involved may become no more than an expensive hobby. Thus it is necessary to produce horses with the most promising talent for jumping or dressage, as the case may be.

It is therefore important to be able at an early stage to judge effectively different qualities in horses that are of special significance for jumping. Obviously a breeding organisation such as the Swedish Government Stud at Flyinge which works on the principle of choosing breeding-stock for its

different abilities has a fair chance of being successful. The importance of the CNS, the organs of sense and the muscles for the jumping horse's balance, canter action and the effort of jumping has been explained. As these functions ultimately decide how good a jumper a horse can become, we would like to outline the different ways in which a horse's talents for show jumping can be tested. Further, we present points of view of how, through early and correct training of the young horse, one should be able to develop and fix effectively the horse's special talent for jumping.

Conventional principles for breeding

The Swedish half-bred horse has a fine reputation all over the world — not only as an all-rounder but also as a competing horse. In international dressage especially, considerable successes have been achieved. The explanation lies in the principles laid down for the breeding of horses by the Government Stud in co-operation with the Association for Breeding the Swedish Warm-blood Horse.

The warm-blood horse in the defence forces

During the first decades of the 20th century the breeding of half-bred horses prospered. The Forces required good horses and the breeders could meet most of their demands. With the insistence on compulsory examination of stallions, keeping of stud books, Government-owned studs and economic aid from the Government to help in the import of breeding animals, the Swedish half-bred or warm-blood horse attained a high standard. The goal was to produce easily fed, hard horses with strong constitutions. Any horses which did not reach the required standard were discarded — and the standard was judged by thorough veterinary examinations, cross-country tests and by using the horses on manoeuvres. In this manner, the all-rounder horse, known today as the Swedish warm-blood, was created. The number of horses needed in the Forces diminished and in consequence, so did the number of brood mares. The most valuable mares were, however, retained, and thus a consolidation of the stock of mares was achieved which further increased the quality of the Swedish warm-blood horse.

New markets
In spite of the fact that the Forces today have no horses, there is a relatively good market for half-bred horses. The reason is the rapid development in the use of horses for riding. Many horses have also been exported, and the Swedish warm-blood horse has shown its considerable qualities in international dressage.

Judging conformation and constitution
The conformation of the Swedish warm-blood horse is considered to be of the greatest importance. However, this line of thought can be rather dangerous and the leading breeding societies have, since the beginning of 1950, started to recruit breeding stock from families of brood-mares that have shown inherent qualities for competition work. Because the Forces no longer keep horses, it has proved difficult to test effectively the constitutions and other qualities of the horses produced, and compulsory efficiency tests similar to those in other European countries for warm-blood stallions have been introduced.
The qualities of brood-mares are, on the whole, only judged at exhibitions and award classes. Thus few opportunities to judge anything but conformation are offered and, consequently, the merits of a well-made animal chiefly decide the value of breeding. The importance of tests for efficiency has been discussed, but unfortunately, these ideas have not yet produced any practical results.

The principles of selection

Many books have touched upon the complicated problem of how to produce horses with good jumping ability. Many breeders have tried to turn out the ideal jumping horse, and some have succeeded, but it is important that both stallion and mare should possess the ability or flair for jumping, whether in the arena or for eventing. Importance has been attached to certain points of conformation and the stud has also tried to produce strong and hard horses.

The horse with a "jumping head"
We have learnt that, besides a good exterior and a strong constitution, additional requirements must be met — the horse must have a "jumping head". The horse with this quality is different from the average horse, having especially good balance and muscle co-ordination, quick reactions, the ability to judge distance correctly and an effective jumping technique.
It has been established that the "jumping head" is inherited and to be found particularly in certain blood lines. By an understanding of the existing breeding principles with the special tests of ability, it should be possible to map out more clearly the various qualities that make an outstanding jumping horse. The breeding should, in other words, be directed in various ways towards combining such special qualities.

The Swedish warm-blood as a suitable jumper
Several Swedish teams have already attained worthwhile international successes. Thus the Swedish warm-blood should be a suitable type of horse for the production of promising material for show jumping, as should any other warm-blood breed of horse having suitable blood lines.

Test of ability for better selection
As far as breeds like the Thoroughbred or the American Trotter are concerned, their performance in competitions has for centuries been decisive in

choosing the right sort of breeding animals. As far as the breed of warm-blood horses goes, it is not quite so easy to choose suitable breeding animals with special talents of the kind required for jumping. There are many difficulties, but the test of ability could be a solution. As regards the breeding of other domestic animals, we have for a long time had them under subjective control for their suitability as breeding animals and we have been able to judge them objectively for such qualities as are of importance for their particular range of use. Combined with veterinary control, efficiency tests should give a sounder basis for the selection of stock, including the Swedish warm-blood horse.

Test of ability

Fundamentally, there are two ways of finding out the qualities of a horse for jumping:
1) Statistics of the results of competitions.
2) Test of ability.
The statistic examinations of competition results have, however, one great weakness. It takes too long a time before a sufficient number of off-spring have been able to compete to give a true idea of the parents' ability to pass on jumping ability. A further limitation is that the result obtained is influenced by the different riders' and trainers' ability to school and train young horses. The long interval between generations of horses underlines the need for finding methods of selection — objective tests of the horse's ability to judge and lift himself, effective back action, fast reactions, good muscle co-ordination and other factors are decisive for a first-class jumping horse. By testing parents as well as offspring, one will be able to analyse more effectively to what degree the various qualities have been inherited. If such tests of ability can be made effective, one has obtained a useful instrument of selection for breeding stock.

Making the test of ability
At the Government Stud at Flyinge loose jumping is done by routine in order to train and test the jumping ability of the future breeding stallions. By watching carefully and studying the way in which the horses jump different types of fences, it is possible to get a good general idea of their jumping technique. If, however, one wants to study such qualities as judgement and ability to lift, back action, ability of self-correction, time of reaction, etc., the above mentioned method must be developed into a standardized and effective test. How to make such a test achieve a proper result? Before this question can be definitely answered, naturally certain trials are necessary. It appears that the tests of ability should be carried out as loose jumping under standardized conditions. With the system of breeding as practised at present, the horses should be tested as three-year-olds.

The eye is not sufficient
If one wants to study fast movements in detail — canter, jumping technique, etc. — the eye is not sufficient. The human eye is too uncertain an instrument and misses a lot of essential information. Further it is impossible to remember a visual impression in detail for a sufficient period of time to make comparisons of the horse's technique at different moments.
One way of solving this problem is to film the horses in action.
By marking certain spots on the horses it will then be possible, by taking measurements on the film, to compile interesting information of various talents. Thus one gets the opportunity to make objective comparisons between the jumping techniques of different horses and of the same horse's technique on different occasions.

Repeated standardized jumping exercises
In allowing each horse, during the test, to jump several times — for example a high fence — it will be possible to study his ability to choose every time the most suitable line of take-off. This also gives an idea of where to put an aid fence in order to indicate the take-off line that best suits the

horse. When the conditions have been established in this manner, the horses' way of jumping can be filmed in an ideal set-up.
By using the aid fence, the distance to the test fence can be shortened, thus provoking the horse to show — amongst other things — his ability to lift himself. On the other hand, if the take-off is lengthened, other qualities can be studied — impulsion, for example.

The films give information and documentation
On the films one can take measurements and so get important information about the horse's jumping technique without having forced him to jump especially large fences. If the test is carried out over other types of fence, one will get additional information, for instance how a horse reacts to the massive appearance of an oxer, his ability to execute a collected canter during the approach, etc.
This method should also be used when selecting competition horses.
In this way many mistakes could be avoided and only gifted horses would then be trained for the big competitions.

Training of young horses

The discussion about tests of ability is linked with another interesting and possibly controversial question — the training of the young, unbroken horse. The development within international show jumping makes ever greater demands on the top horses — particularly regarding quick reaction, muscle co-ordination and balance, also hardness and obedience. The fences are increasingly frequently built up to the maximum limit, the distance between fences and in the combinations appears more difficult, etc. The international jumping horse of today is, in short, a very great artist.

It should be started in time . . .
We know that most functions of the nervous system can be trained — the muscle co-ordination, the balance, the effective co-ordination of the impressions of sense, etc. In order to achieve maximum results from the horse's inherited ability, we in Sweden feel his training must begin when a foal and as a young horse. It is namely the young individual who is especially susceptible to various types of technique training. In most sports this has been practised for a long time. To reach the top in, for instance, gymnastics, diving and skiing, the technique training must be started at an early age.

. . . and this applies to the horse as well
The importance of the early training of jumping horses has not had sufficient attention. Many breeders and horse-owners are, certainly justifiably, hesitant about early training of their horses. Young horses tire very easily and their hearts can be overstrained without the trainer being aware of it. The result is sourness and refusal to do what is asked of them. Their bones are also not developed. Too many promising young horses are ruined annually by owners, trainers and riders being in too much of a hurry. This, however, need not be the case if one pursues a sensible technique training and avoids exposing the horse to undue

efforts. The principles mentioned here must not be confused with riding too soon or hard training, which is distinctly dangerous for the young horse. It is considered quite natural not to train a horse for jumping until he has been schooled for riding. However, even a very skilled rider will make it difficult for the young horse to develop an effective jumping technique; much could be gained if, before he was broken, the future jumping horse could be given several years to develop and establish all the reflexes that are so important for jumping.

Quietly, skilfully and consistently
It has to be strongly emphasized that all training of foals and young horses must be pursued quietly, skilfully and consistently. Stress and overexertion easily lead to psychological and physical damage.
It is of great importance that the training is pursued in such a way that the horses establish a correct technique. It is virtually impossible to correct a faulty movement pattern that is learnt early on and becomes established. The training must therefore be designed individually in order to preserve the special ability of the individual horse.

The foal

In Sweden, the training of the foal begins by letting the mare and foal be put together in undulating paddocks. The foal soon learns to look out for stones, stumps and other objects. As soon as possible, the foal should be allowed to follow its mother on short rides, provided there are fields and tracks entirely free of traffic. Gradually these rides should take place in a terrain that brings out reactions in order to make the foal jump minor natural obstacles, like logs and ditches. The foal thus learns to look out, and its ability to co-ordinate and its independence increase.
It should never be over-taxed. The object of this training is only to develop reactions. Some days it should learn to go as a lead horse.

Contact with humans
As soon as the foal is weaned, it has to learn to

obey orders and listen to voices, in co-ordination with long-reining. In this way, contact with humans is established, which is of great importance for its future development.
The foal can also be groomed and taught to lead and since the farrier will attend to the foal's feet, the sooner it allows its legs to be handled, the better. However, a foal should never be tied up, since very young horses tend to panic very easily, and it should never be left alone in its box. If, for some reason, the mare has to be taken away from the foal, it must have a companion. It is also important that the foal gets to know the person who will be in charge of its care and education.

Reward and reproof
To facilitate later training, the foal should be taught to appreciate a reward and learn from a reprimand. This is necessary and makes it possible to influence the foal. It is important that all exercises should be fun as this will develop the wish for co-ordination.

Technique, physique and balance
During the winter months the foal should be allowed out-of-doors as much as possible. It gets new experience from games with its fellows and plunging in the snow, it can give vent to its energy and will develop physically by training its muscles on its own. In the first year, the foal's balance is thus developed and the association with human beings begun.
One must, however, look out for negative reactions. They are noticeable in reduced play, lack of appetite and peevishness. At the first sign of such symptoms, the training must be eliminated and the foal allowed a period of rest.

The yearling

The Swedish method of developing future show jumpers is discussed on the following pages. The growth of the horse as a yearling is very rapid. One must therefore constantly bear in mind that schooling is pursued without overworking the horse. Each jumping exercise should be preceded by a short warming-up period — for instance long reining — which reduces the risk of injuries.

Jumping a standard fence
Through loose jumping the yearling should learn to negotiate a simple standard fence that is later used as an aid fence during the training which follows. It is thus very important to encourage the yearling to jump it willingly and confidently. The yearling should also learn to go over cavaletti. Consequently, the fence and cavaletti training should, all the time, be pursued simultaneously. Cavaletti exercises should be planned individually and will not be discussed here.

Continuous repetitions
It is impossible for the yearling himself to judge where to take-off. The standard fence therefore aids him to choose a correct take-off place for the fence used in training. The height of the fence must never exceed 2 ft 6 in; a rail on the ground either 1 ft 6 in or 2 ft 6 in away from the fence will help train his eye for correct distances.
By consequent repetition of jumping the combinations of fences, the horse's brain is working all the time during the approach and the take-off and receiving messages from the different organs of sense. Through constant training, such information is firmly impressed on the memory and the horse learns to co-ordinate the canter action and the judgement of distance at one and the same time, thus making a well adjusted leap. In this way one gets the opportunity to teach the horse to judge where to take-off and what elevation and impulsion is required.

Take away the aid fence — retain the pattern
When one considers that the horse's jumping technique is well established, the aid fence, which must never be higher than 1 ft 6 in, is removed. Now, when the young horse again approaches the fence, the CNS continuously still registers the impulses coming from the different sense organs.

Because the CNS has imprinted how these impulses should be felt — if the fence is cleared — the horse is better able to co-ordinate his judgement of distance and his canter action, so as to take-off at the correct spot and in the correct way. To gain permanent effects from schooling, each exercise must cover both repetition of the preceding exercise and the teaching of new ones. From the beginning, to prevent an eventual one-sidedness, the horse must be trained daily both on left and right tracks.

Physical training and natural external effects

The purpose is still simply to school and improve the yearling's nervous system and organs of sense. An additional advantage is that there is naturally a certain training of muscles and the capacity of heart and lungs. The horse is thus little by little prepared for his future development in impulsion and stamina.

Now is the time for the test of ability

With such early schooling in jumping, it should be possible to do the test of ability when the horse is still a yearling. Through repeated tests one can also note the effect of the training. Experience shows that the speed of the training to learn, in co-ordination with the training of movements, varies with different horses. Some learn relatively slowly but, even so, show promise of becoming successful jumpers.

The two-year-old

As a two-year-old the jumping horse has reached the age when trotting and race horses are already in full training and often make their first starts. However, the development of the half-bred is much slower, and he is definitely not ready to be put to a real form of training. From a veterinary and medical point of view it is therefore not advisable to start breaking the half-bred before the age of two and a half years.

Among trotting and racing people, opinion is divided as to how early to start the actual training. As a rule they realize the importance of technique training and it is often begun at the

yearling stage. This has not always been successful, as the training has often not been limited to pure technique training. Too many horses are ruined yearly by being put into full training at a time when they are not sufficiently developed, physically or psychologically.

Continued jumping

The two-year-old should develop his jumping technique further and one can now start the training with loose jumping over more difficult types of fence. This does not mean that the fences should be raised to greater heights; instead they should be varied as much as possible. Besides different types of fence, the horse will now get to know various combinations. The exercises should be repeated more often but in such a way that the joy of jumping should be encouraged.

The three-year-old

During the third year, the schooling already described should be continued. The three-year-old is becoming more sure of balance, how to use himself and other jumping techniques. Besides this development of the various nervous functions, it is now time to get the horse into full training to improve his condition. Technique training is no longer sufficient. The horse must also be schooled and systematically prepared for the exertions he will be exposed to as a competition horse. This is best done by taking him, as a lead horse, on gradually longer rides and, naturally, let him be with other horses on undulating terrain. The fences should not exceed 3 ft 6 in and the youngster must not be jumped too often.

Condition and strength

By getting him into condition the three-year-old is basically ready for schooling under a rider, which period should not be started until he is four years old. It is, of course, advisable at this stage to accustom the horse to saddle, snaffle, etc. By careful mounting and dismounting — preferably in the riding school — the young horse learns to accept the weight of a rider.

The four-year-old

When the horse is four years old, he is ridden-in. He gets accustomed to the aids of the rider and is taught fundamental dressage before he starts jumping under a rider. During this time, however, loose jumping should be continued, even if schooling under a rider is occasionally pursued.

With a rider over fences

Mounted by a rider the horse is gradually allowed to jump different fences and learns to compensate for this rather difficult moment in his training. By this time, the horse has a well-founded loose jumping technique and soon gets to know how to cope with the weight of the rider, balance, etc. in his action and jumping, so that he keeps up the effective technique which he learnt earlier on.

Co-ordination for development

For centuries, many different systems for training and riding horses have been developed. Based on tradition and considerable experience these different schools of thought and practice contain a vast knowledge of horses and riding. The best trainers and riders have intuitive ability to be able to modify their chosen system to suit the individual horse.

The question which confronts us today is to compare the methods of the different schools for practical purposes in order to be able to judge what is "right" or "wrong".

The film material in this book shows that there are great similarities in the techniques of the different horses, despite the fact that they have been developed in different countries and the horses are trained and ridden according to different basic principles. We need, therefore, to find ways of studying these common traits in order to be able to choose the right horses and then to develop the best methods of training them. Continued research and close co-operation with leading breeders, trainers and riders should cultivate, preserve and develop ideas of the greatest value.

Select Bibliography

Bürger, Udo: Vollendete Reitkunst, Paul Parey, Berlin, 1961

Carlsöö, S.: Människans rörelse, PA-rådet, Stockholm 1968

Crawell, D.: American Horses, Bonanza Books, N.Y., 1951

d'Endrödy, A. L.: Give your horse a chance, J. A. Allen & Co., London, 2nd ed., 1967

Evarts, E. V. (Chairman): Central Control of Movement, Neurosci. Res. Program Bull. 1971, 9:1

Fillis, J.: Grundsätze der Dressur und Reitkunst, 3 aufl. Gustaf Goebel, Stuttgart, 1905

Ganong, W. F.: Medical physiology
Lange Medical Publication, Los Altos Cal. 1969

Goubeaux & Barrier: The exterior of the horse, 2nd ed.
J. B. Lippincott, Philadelphia 1904

Gray, J.: Animal locomotion, 1st ed.
William Clowes & Sons Ltd, London & Beccles 1968

Gregory, W. K.: Notes on the principles of quadrupedal locomotion and on the mechanism of the limbs in hoofed animals. Ann. N.Y. Acad. Sci., 1912. *22*, 267—294

Grzimek, B.: Versuche über das Farbsehen von Pflanzenessern
Z. Tierpsychol., 1952, *9*, 23—39

Grzimek, B.: Die Händigkeit bei Pferden
Z. Tierpsychol., 1949. *6*, 414—432

Hance, J. E.: Better horsemanship
Country Life Ltd, London, 1948

Hance, J. E.: School for Horse and Rider
Country Life Ltd, London, 1932

Hayes, M. H.: The points of the horse, 7th rev. ed.
W. Thacker & Co, London, 1969

Hontang, M.: Psychologie du cheval — sa personnalité
Payot Paris, 1954

Hope, C. E. G., & Harris, C.: Riding technique in pictures, 3rd ed. J. A. Allen & Co., London 1968

Ixer, E.: Course building
Show-jumping Year, Cassell, London 1957

Klimke, R.: Cavaletti, 2. Aufl.
Franckh'sch verlagshandlung, W. Keller & Co., Stuttgart 1969

Lewis, B.: Riding, Garden City, N.Y., 1939

Lithander, L.: Dressyrridning — hoppning, 2a uppl. Bonniers, 1967

MacConaill, M. A., & Basmajian, J. V.: Muscles and Movements
The William & Wilkins Co., Baltimore, 1969

Marcenak, L. N., & Aublet, H.: Encyclopédie du cheval
Librairie Maloine, S. A., Paris, 1964

Muybridge, E.: Animals in locomotion
L. S. Brown Ed., Dover Publications, N.Y., 1957

Nauckhoff, V.: Hästen, dess natur, skötsel & vård
Bonniers, Sthlm, 1896

Nissen, J.: Springen und was dazugehört
Hoffman Verlag, Heidenheim, 1968

Ottoson, D.: Nervsystemets fysiologi, Natur & Kultur, 1970

Palmer, R. D.: Development of a differentiated handedness
Psychol. Bull., 1964, vol 62, no 4, 257—272

Polyak, S.: The vertebrate visual system
The University of Chicago Press, 1957

von Redwitz, M.: Die Grundsätze der Dressur, Berlin, 1914

von Redwitz, M.: Springen und Geländereiten, Berlin, 1914

Roberts, T. D. M.: Neurophysiology of postural mechanismus
Butterworths, London, 1967

Rooney, J. R.: Biomechanics of lameness in horses
William & Wilkins Co., Baltimore, 1969

Sidney, S.: Book of the horse, rev. ed.
Cassell & Co. Ltd., London, Paris, & Melbourne, 1893

Sisson, S., & Grossman, J. D.: Anatomy of the domestic animals
W. B. Saunders Co., Philadelphia, 1953

Smith, F.: Manual of veterinaray physiology, 5th ed.
Alex Eger, Chicago, 1921

Smythe, R. H.: Veterinary ophthalmology
Baillère, Tindall & Cox, London, 1956

Smythe, R. H.: Animal vision. What animals see
Herbert Jenkins, London, 1961

Smythe, R. H.: Horses in action, Country Life Ltd., London 1963

Smythe, R. H.: The mind of the horse
Country Life Ltd., London, 1963

Steinkraus, W.: Riding and jumping
J. A. Allen & Co., London, 1961

Stillman, J. D. B.: The horses in motion
James R. Osgood & Co., Boston, 1882

Svenska Armén: Ridinstruktion, 1940 års uppl.

Talbot-Ponsonby, J.: Technique in show-jumping
Show-jumping year 2
Cassell, London, 1959

Walls, G. L.: The vertebrate eye
Cranbrook Institute of Sci., 1942

Williams, D.: Show-jumping
Faber & Faber, London, 1968

Wooldridge, D. E.: Hjärnans maskineri, Aldus, 1967

Training and Riding Jumping Horses

All jumping horses have different talents for jumping and all riders have different natural ways of riding. It stands to reason, therefore, that the training of different teams and partnerships cannot be standardized but must be practised individually, depending on the qualifications of rider and horse. It is also obvious that no universal rules or advice for training or riding can be laid down. An experienced and successful trainer or rider, however, has an extensive "know-how" — they know intuitively "how to do it". They know what essentially to observe in the action of horse and rider and they have a good idea of how to correct mistakes in the action of the horse and how to develop and improve it.

Space does not permit a detailed description of training patterns for different teams. In spite of great differences between various teams, there are certain features common to successful horses and riders. Lars Sederholm, the author of this chapter, is obliged to limit himself to giving a general survey, based on considerable practical experience, of his own personal opinion of training and riding jumping horses.

It has often been established that there are many different ways of training a horse to make him successful. However, three things are common to all prominent riders — they get the horse properly balanced, they have a fine feeling for the rhythm of the horse and they drive the horse forward during the last few strides before the fence.

There are two basic elements in training:

1. The training programme.
2. The rider's behaviour in the saddle.

The training programme

This section will deal with:

- ☐ Work on the flat.
- ☐ Cavaletti exercises.
- ☐ Jumping fences.

Besides these exercises one must consider the horse's general well-being and routine.

Work on the flat

This training aims to give the horse the right balance for jumping and the development of the muscles. Many riders have a natural "feel" for jumping. Such a good "feel" brings out the best in the horse — particularly if the horse naturally moves in a way which corresponds with the rider's style. The rider who masters the horse on the flat can, in certain situations, improve the horse's

ability to make use of his resources and therefore has greater chances of succeeding with several horses.

It is quite easy to see how a horse has been trained by studying how his muscles have developed. Personally, I prefer a horse with well developed muscles along the upper part of the body. If a horse has a strong underside to his neck, he will eventually become weaker behind the saddle. To be able to jump well, he then needs support from a strong hand and a martingale. Thus, the muscles along the crest and along the loins behind the saddle should be built up. This is to enable the horse to carry his rider in a correct, strong and sound manner and not to "give" to the rider's weight.

Development of the muscles

The best way of developing the muscles on the upper part of the body is to drive him from "behind" with his head and neck lowered. To achieve this, the rider must ride so that the horse is well balanced with the hindlegs "well under". When the horse moves with head and neck lowered and held forward, the whole top line will stretch. If the rider, with his horse in this position, makes half-halts and shortens the stride, it will be seen after a time how the muscles of the hind-quarters, back and neck successively develop. The rider who is striving to make his horse jump in a correct manner will realize the advantage of this, as these muscles are of great importance for the horse's jumping ability.

Sometimes it has been suggested that a lowered head and neck, during exercise on the flat, would mean too much work on the forehand. To avoid this, it is important that the horse puts his hind-legs well under the body. The advantage of a low head will clearly be seen when the horse jumps a fence. He lowers head and neck in order to use the back muscles better when the hindlegs push. It is of utmost importance for the trainer to know what he has to observe during the actual jump, so that he can consistently plan work on the flat. Personally, I maintain that work on the flat must be parallel with that over fences — that is, training on the flat is never finished. I have also found that if anything goes wrong during work on the flat, a little jumping may put it right. Naturally, it works the other way round, but one must use ordinary common sense.

Cavaletti

When communication has been established between rider and horse, the latter should be started over cavaletti and bars lying on the ground. This

training exercise implies the following:
1) For the first time the horse finds something in the way and tries instinctively to avoid touching the obstacle in front of him. This instinct of self-preservation must be retained, as it helps the rider during subsequent training when it comes to negotiating fences faultlessly.
2) Trotting over the bars builds up important muscles, as the steps become higher than normal.
3) Provided that the bars are placed at intervals suitable to the horse's stride, he begins to develop a good rhythm and this is necessary for helping rider and horse to act as one unit when jumping.

Jumping
All the different phases of the development, from the beginning of the cavaletti exercises to jumping fairly large fences cannot be dealt with in detail in this section. To begin with, the horse must be taken over many different fences, so that later on he can approach any type of fence without fear. The horse must not be allowed to take liberties. If he does, the type or height of the fence must be changed immediately to make him respect it. Here the rider must show great patience. How long it will take before one can begin to judge the horse's jumping technique all depends on his natural ability. The idea is to confront him with every imaginable type of fence and make him canter towards them with respect and self-confidence.

Straight up-and-down and wide fences
The two main types of fence which the horse must learn to jump are the straight up-and-down and wide fences.
Until he has learnt to distinguish between these two types, he will never be successful in competitions. The rider's contribution varies — the more difficult the fences, the more distinct the aids he must give.
Straight up-and-down fences
These demand an earlier take-off than the wide ones and also require the rider to judge distance more precisely. If a horse is allowed to do what he wants, he can easily get too near the fence.
Wide fences
These are usually filled out with bars, hurdles, coloured mats or rugs and sharpen the horse's instinct for self-preservation. Thus the rider can approach the fence with more confidence and give the horse more courage. Owing to the construction of the fence, the horse will find it easier. A

bold approach often means a better and more powerful leap. The rider urges his horse forward, but as he looks at the fence with a certain respect, he doesn't easily respond to the rider's legs. The result is that, between the approach to the fence and the aids to urge him forward, the horse's collection is increased. This puts the horse's legs in a position which makes him lift himself well and he then jumps the fence with plenty of impulsion.

The difference between techniques when jumping straight up-and-down fences and wide fences can best be studied from pictures of different riders and horses when jumping different fences. A horse can sometimes clear a straight up-and-down fence, even if he gets too near, or a wide one if he takes off too early. As a rule, however, he fails on both occasions.

The horse's general well-being

Up to now, I have only mentioned the technical aspects of jumping. During the whole period of training one must, of course, make sure that the horse's general condition is satisfactory. Besides the technical training, the horse must be happy and contented as well as attentive in his work. In England and Ireland it is considered useful to let young horses hunt. Even at an early stage, they get the feeling of going forward and clearing the obstacle in front — the only way to keep up with the other horses. But one gets more out of a horse when hunting if he has learnt a bit about jumping beforehand. He should be able to clear 1m fences without fear.

It is important that the rider should be able to inspire his horse with a liking for sport and competition work and to handle him correctly during cross-country rides. A good track is desirable — preferably grass — with different types of fences, hurdles, ditches, gates and, if possible, banks as well.

It is important that the horse be taken for good, vigorous rides together with other horses two or three times weekly. These rides should be made as attractive as possible and in suitable terrain. Provided that the horse is in good condition, he will develop fast and enjoy his training.

Routine for jumping competitors

As soon as the horse has begun to take part in competitions one must remember that every now and then he needs a change from the daily routine. I believe in taking the horse out for occasional quiet canters before the hunting season starts — a few times every month, even during the season. Not only will his form improve, but he enjoys cantering along in the company of other horses. The track must be good, and one should choose a suitable day and time for the ride; obviously a brisk morning is better than a hot summer's day. When the horse shows good form as a competitor, hunting should be stopped. Accidents can happen and a promising show jumper is very valuable. When he has progressed beyond the beginner's stage, his life becomes very specialized. Nice canters in a moderate tempo are healthy, but the horse should not be allowed to go too fast. I further believe that short spells of rest are better for a competing horse than a long unbroken period. If the horse is idle for too long, the muscles begin to decline and it will be difficult to take time to rebuild his competition form successfully. However, it is recommended that, once a year, the horse should be let down and given a complete rest.

Riding

The role of the rider is just as important as a well-planned training programme. I have found that the rider with the most orthodox seat does not necessarily make the fewest mistakes. Primarily what counts is the ability to keep the horse well balanced and ensure that the forward impulsion is co-ordinated with the feeling for the rhythm of the horse. If the rider himself has a good rhythm, he can allow his horse free movements in each stride — the horse then gets a feeling of confidence and trusts his rider. If the horse is ridden in this way over low fences, he will sometimes take off too soon — or get too close — but he will, all the same, jump the fence satisfactorily.

The consequences of lack of rhythm

The rider who lacks rhythm is usually too stiff to follow his horse's movements. The natural ability

of the horse is thus restrained — he often has to adapt himself to the faults of the rider. The horse is disturbed in his normal way of doing his best and cannot concentrate on jumping faultlessly. He will be on his guard, his movements become jerky and he is afraid of going on to jump the obstacle.

The rider's "eye" helps him to judge distance

It has often been said that certain riders have an inborn judgement of correct distance and that it is impossible to acquire this through training. This may often be true, but an inferior judgement of distance can be improved and a good one made even better with increased experience and continuous training. I have also found that riders with a well developed rhythm improve their judgement of distance more quickly than others. The reason for this is that the young rider who, with feel and a sense of rhythm, riding a young, inexperienced horse over beginner's fences, will soon find that he can approach the fence without anxiety as the horse will clear it faultlessly, even if he jumps off at the wrong place. If the rider knows that the horse can do this over low fences, he will soon find that he can influence the horse either to lengthen or shorten the strides at the beginning of the approach to the fence.

However, the rider who lacks rhythm will find that his own stiffness will cause corresponding faults in the horse, who then takes off in a jerky manner — if at all. If the horse gets too near the fence he very often lands in the middle of it. If this happens repeatedly, the rider becomes uncertain and tries to improve his approach.

Because of these efforts he unfortunately very often gets even stiffer and loses still more of the rhythm.

Maybe the rider can clear smaller fences in this manner — but he will never be able to develop the horse's movements properly, which is necessary in advanced show jumping. Here, the fences are often so big as to demand the greatest effort from the horse.

Riding young horses

Riders without natural rhythm should avoid jumping young horses. The horse will soon develop complexes because of the rider's lack of co-ordination. There are, however, horses with such an outstanding sense of rhythm that it can be transferred to the rider, but these are the exceptions. Therefore, riders with inferior rhythm should train on experienced horses. They should try to feel the rhythm of the horse and learn from him. In most cases, though, this must not continue for a long period, as the horse will rapidly deteriorate.

Riders with good rhythm — even with limited experience — can train young horses for jumping. In fact, young riders with natural rhythm, balance and forward urge are the best fitted to teach young horses during the first phases of training. A more experienced rider will notice the faults made by the horse and will correct them, and so the horse will not repeat his mistakes. Provided that they are made when the horse is going forward, well balanced, it is useful for him, even at an early stage, to learn to be alert. The advantages of this will become clearly apparent later in life when he is ridden by a more experienced rider who makes him jump high and wide fences. The horse will then approach the fence with wholesome respect and will have the ability to lift himself and jump — determined to clear the fence faultlessly.

The horse needs various forms of assistance from his rider during different stages of development. This is the reason why one finds that riders who are good at training young horses, are rarely successful with experienced horses. On the other hand, there are riders who can handle, develop

and win great competitions on horses which have been trained by others. In other words, you will find very few riders and trainers who can bring their horses from beginner's stage right up to the competitive standard of international competitions.

Riding on the flat

Some riders can train horses successfully on the flat, but not for jumping. This is because they try to change the horse's stride and action according to their own ideas. The dressage rider, for this reason, in many cases adjusts and corrects the horse's stride when instead, he should endeavour to urge him forward whilst keeping him well balanced. The jumping rider, on the other hand, is often happier when urging his horse forward at a suitable tempo. Thus the jumping rider more easily accepts the horse's natural movements and then makes the best of them.

It is my firm belief that the few riders who are able to develop a horse from the very beginning to international class have the same feeling for work on the flat as for jumping. They first study the horse's development on the flat and, on the basis of this, commence the training for jumping fences. They know that because they have given the horse a thorough schooling on the flat, they can demand more of him in his approach to the fence. A successful trainer knows how he wants his horse to jump and also that previous schooling on the flat is essential. This moment consists of, amongst other things, the building up of the back muscles, to get the horse going "straight", trying to make him put his hindlegs well under, etc. All this gradually changes the horse. During this training

the rider must "give orders" to the horse all the time. The demands of the rider must always be adapted to the actual level of the horse's education. When the horse is sufficiently physically developed and psychologically obedient to follow the rider, he is ready to begin jumping fences.

Ideally, the horse should automatically react to the aids of his rider. If he does, he will — as long as he is urged forward and kept well balanced — have his concentration directed forwards towards the fence. This, along with respect for the fence, induces the horse to make an effort to clear it. In fact, it is only when the horse is completely concentrated on the fences that one can expect faultless jumps.

After a jumping competition, one often hears riders say that the horse must obey. They are surprised that he has knocked down a certain fence in spite of a strong restraint before the fence or the one previous to it. The reason is, of course, that the horse paid too much attention to his rider, and this worked against him. He tried to jump in spite of the rider's behaviour, but did not get the same chance of going faultlessly as the concentration was split between the fence and the rider's activities.

Summing up

At the beginning, I pointed out that there are many ways of successfully training a jumping horse. The most important point, however, is for the rider to keep his horse in good spirits and be able to keep him going forward in a well-balanced rhythm. If this can be achieved, both horse and rider should be well on the way towards giving a good account of themselves.

Series of Pictures

for the study of jumping techniques

The European Championships of 1969 were held in the Hickstead Jumping Arena (England). A group from the Veterinary High School in Stockholm was given permission to film the various teams in action. Normal film cameras as well as slow-motion cameras were used — 25 frames per second and 400 frames per second respectively.

1. Series of pictures of individual teams. Here one can study in detail the techniques of the rider and the horse when jumping. The interval between pictures is 1/50th of a second.
2. Comparative series of pictures of three different teams over the same fence. The commencement of this series is the phase of the first part of the take-off, when the forefoot of the leading foreleg is about to leave the ground. The time interval between pictures here is 1/20th of a second. In this way one can study the action of members of the individual teams as well as differences in action between members of the teams.

From the rider's point of view, the picture comments are made by Anders Gernandt and from the veterinary point of view by Ingvar Fredricson and assistants.

From this series of pictures the expert can glean much information. It is, however, impossible to comment in detail on each picture. The purpose of these observations is only to give the reader an example of how the series can be used to study different styles and techniques of riders and horses. The veterinary medical comments refer also to various sections of the text.

David Broome

Born in Wales in 1940 and raised in a family all of whom are in some way connected with horses. His father, Fred Broome, as his advisor, travels with him to competitions. David Broome has been in the limelight of international show jumping since, as a nineteen-year-old, he made his successful début in the Rome Olympiad. He took the bronze medal on the horse Sunsalve. In 1964 he represented England at the Tokyo Olympiad with Jacape. He has been triple European Champion, once on Sunsalve, twice on Mr Softee.

David Broome Mr Softee

Oxer 1.60 × 1.80 m

Typical Broome approach with the seat in the saddle, hands held high and the horse well on the bit.

The horse canters . . .

No change.

The rider's hands are raised and at the same time the position of the horse's head and neck is noticeably altered.

The horse is "free".

The wide fence demands that the rider does not disturb the horse.

The horse brings his hindlegs up.

The rider assists with legs stretched forward.

. . . rhythmically and energetically.

Here the horse knows that he is going correctly — rider and horse in complete harmony.

The hindlegs are now well under the horse's body.

The rider in correct balance.

Horse and rider in complete harmony.

It looks as if the failing parabola could cause the hindlegs to fault.

The landing — well balanced.

The rider prepares a turn to the left. Notice how his weight aids the horse.

David Broome Mr Softee

Upright fence 1.60 m

Canter action with lowered hindquarters.

Hindquarters shifting the centre of gravity.

Forward change. The forehand is lowered before the first phase of the take-off.

The neck is raised. The forefoot has begun to leave the ground from the lowered position.

Impulsion is terminated.

The forelegs bend sufficiently.

The forelegs stretch to prepare for the landing — the point of the toe first on the ground.

Forelegs well apart are necessary on landing, as the horse cannot bend a burdened foreleg.

Going on.

Correct canter to the right.

Going on. The forefeet have left the ground before the hindfeet are put down.

Push-off by the hindlegs. The neck is beginning to stretch.

The joints of the knees and hocks bend . . .

. . . to prevent the hindlegs from dropping.

The hindlegs must be put on the ground quickly . . .

. . . to catch the weight and throw it forward.

Upright fence 1.60 m

David Broome   Top of the Morning

Collection in the take-off — raised head and neck, restraint as the forefeet leave the ground. (See First Part of the Take-off, Reflexes.)

Hollowed back.

Hans-Günther Winkler   Torphy

One ear forwards — one backwards . . .

. . . shows concentration . . .

Åke Hultberg   Magnor

Collection in the take-off — the hindfeet well forward.

A well arched back.

David Broome has obvious troubles mastering the difficult Top of the Morning. He drives forward and restrains at the same time. The hand goes too far back. Observe the position of the elbows.

Winkler, well balanced, has found the right take-off point, taking the fence obliquely from left to right in a confident and cool manner.

Hultberg exercises perfect style on Magnor. Perfect balance and light "give". Note the horse's foreleg technique.

. . . on both fence and rider.

Both ears forward — concentration on the fence.

Impulsion quickly terminated — effect of explosive power. (See Muscles.)

Upright fence 1.60 m

David Broome   Top of the Morning

The problem of balance is diminished by the position of the forelegs. (See the landing.)

Hans-Günther Winkler   Torphy

The rider's centre of gravity being to one side and the front feet close together increases the balance problem.

Åke Hultberg   Magnor

All three riders are well balanced. Winkler straightens his upper body to save the horse from being top heavy. This takes place at the moment of landing, or in the canter stride immediately after. Note that the riders are already looking at the next fence.

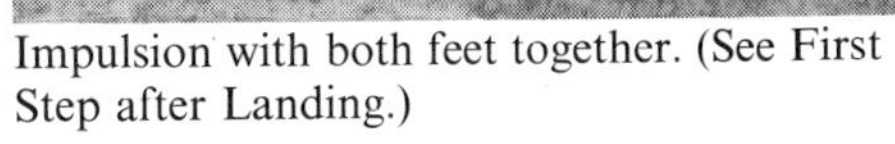

Impulsion with both feet together. (See First Step after Landing.)

An abnormal position of the hindlegs in the canter to the left.

Jonqueres d'Oriola

Born 1920. During the last twenty years the leading show jumping rider in France. He started riding at an early age and won the 1946 Grand Prix in Zurich, his first international competition. In Helsinki he rode Ali Baba and took the gold medal for France. Then, for many years, he looked for another first class jumper and in 1963 bought Lutteus B, sired by the famous stallion Furioso. On Lutteus B he won the gold medal in the individual competitions during the Tokyo Olympiad.

Jonqueres d'Oriola Pomone

Oxer 1.60 × 1.80 m

Powerful approach. The horse reaches towards the fence.

The rider feels that the distance to the fence is just right and allows a long rein.

The horse seems to look hard at the take-off hurdle and "brakes" imperceptibly.

Back taut. The rider's hand slides back a little.

Now comes the "give" (yielding) of the reins — when the rider is sure that the front legs are over.

Loose jumping — where is the rider?

Horse and rider prepare for the landing, whereby the rein is slightly lengthened.

There is no question here of the seat bumping into the saddle.

The rider's leg well forward where it works best to urge the horse forward.

The horse responds to the rider's effective urging with his hindlegs well under him.

A most effective take-off. The rider is correctly balanced.

The rider throws himself forward, but the hand moves further back.

Observe the rider's leg. No rider in the world keeps his leg in the correct position like d'Oriola.

The upper body begins to straighten up.

The horse lands smoothly. Note the position of the pasterns. The horse is free to use his hindleg technique to the full.

The landing is clean, light hand, the leg in an absolutely correct position for effective impulsion towards the next fence.

Upright fence 1.45 m

Jonqueres d'Oriola   Galantérie

The forehand is too close and demands a relatively big angle of elevation. (See the First Part of the Take-off.)

d'Oriola has tried to shift the centre of gravity backwards by raising Galantérie's neck and head. (See the First Part of the Take-off.)

Åke Hultberg   El-Vis

The forehand further away — lower elevation angle is necessary.

The hindlegs wide apart means a smart take-off.

Lutz Merkel   Sperber

Prominently arched back.

d'Oriola gets too close and is clearly forced to restrain the horse at the take-off.
Hultberg's yielding ("give") is too generous, even if the horse jumps higher over the fence than the other horses. His foot in the stirrup is too far back compared with the others. The equilibrium is therefore somewhat disturbed.

The front legs are insufficiently bent. (See Reflexes.)

The forelegs are well drawn up — the take-off could have been closer.

The forelegs are drawn up just as much as is necessary — and at the right moment.

Upright fence 1.45 m

Jonqueres D'Oriola   Galantérie

Risk of a mistake — d'Oriola turns round.

Åke Hultberg   El-Vis

Forelegs widely separated — diminishes the risk of problems of balance.

Lutz Merkel   Sperber

Risk of a mistake — Merkel turns round.

d'Oriola and Merkel are wondering if their horses have touched the bar and so collected faults. Unnecessary, but it happens so quickly that it doesn't disturb the rider's balance and concentration on the next fence.

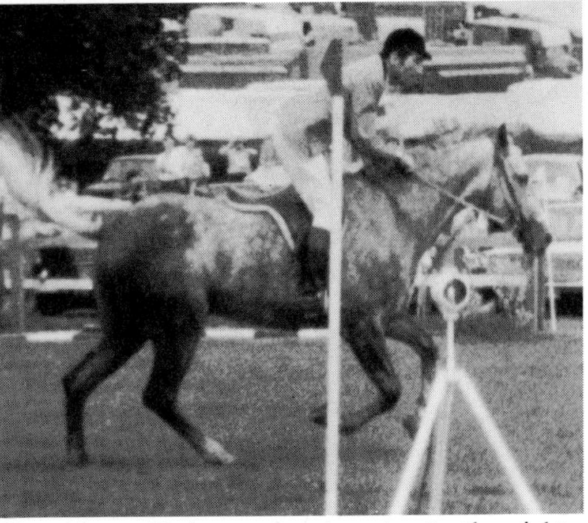

The risk avoided — correct canter to the right.

The centre of gravity is well forward.

El-Vis, with both hindfeet nearly together, has plenty of impulsion. (See The First Stride After Landing.)

An abnormal position of the hindlegs in a canter to the right.

Raimondo d'Inzeo

Born in 1925 in Italy, now officer in the Corps de Carabinière. He started riding very early. As a twelve-year-old, he cleared fences up to 1.70m, and four years later he rode in a steeplechase. He started his international jumping career in 1950 and has since shown his skill by winning with a great number of different horses, amongst others Possillipo, The Quiet Man, Merano, Hack On, Gowran Girl, and Litargerio. At the Stockholm Olympics, he won the silver medal on Merano. In Rome he was again a winner and got the individual gold medal on Possillipo.

Raimondo d'Inzeo Bellevue

Upright fence 1.60 m

The rider in perfect balance with his horse moving at a fast canter.

Powerful pressure with the leg — a bit too far back — indicates that the rider is too far away from the point of take-off.

The pressure is increased.

At the same time the hand goes slightly back and the seat begins to lift.

The rider is trying to disturb the horse as little as possible, knowing that the take-off is too far back.

Acrobatic style, but the balance is right.

. . . and the partnership lands close to the cleared obstacle (well done in a tight situation).

The horse is turning and preparing for the next fence.

Ideal balance.

Still perfect style. The horse is allowed to stretch as much as he wants to.

The upper body forward, the hand towards the hip.

The take-off too far from the fence.

Because of the long take-off, the horse cannot use his back correctly.

The landing obviously begins early . . .

The turn towards the next fence has already begun.

The horse canters undisturbed towards the new fence.

Oxer 1.55 × 1.75 m

Jonqueres d'Oriola   Pomone

The action of the forelegs is similar in all the horses, although the action of the hindlegs varies.

Raimondo d'Inzeo   Bellevue

Take-off away from the fence . . .

David Broome   Mr Softee

First the horses: Pomone jumps with the best back action, Bellevue with an acceptable action and Mr Softee with none at all. Note that the styles of Broome and d'Inzeo are, on the whole, similar. However, d'Inzeo's hand remains in the same place all the time, as compared with the other riders.

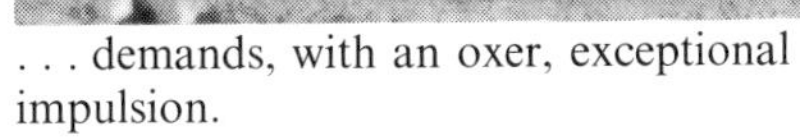
. . . demands, with an oxer, exceptional impulsion.

. . . give a wide angle of elevation.

Oxer 1.55 × 1.75 m

Jonqueres d'Oriola   Pomone

Raimondo d'Inzeo   Bellevue

Early stretched forelegs.

Landing near the fence. (See The Landing.)

David Broome   Mr Softee

Mr Softee's great elevation in the take-off . . .

. . . results in a steep landing.

All riders have a good balance. The landing is always "deep" after a wide fence, and, as the pictures show, the riders must straighten the upper body more than usual when landing.

The bent neck gives increased power to the impulsion of the hindlegs. (See Reflexes.)

The stride after landing is increased. (See The First Stride After Landing.)

Harvey Smith

Born in Yorkshire in 1938. He started taking part in smaller competitions when he finished school. In 1958 he was seen all over England on bigger occasions. His first well-known horse was Farmer's Boy which he bought for only £40. With this horse he took part in his first international competition in Dublin and drew great attention to himself when he helped the English team to win the Nation's Cup. Since then he has been at the top and has won more first prizes than most others.

Harvey Smith Archie

Wall 1.65 m

Even if the rider has his seat in the saddle, his foot is, during the approach, a little too far back.

The horse's neck and head are noticeably high.

The horse seems to look hard at the highest point of the fence in order to decide instinctively the height of the jump.

The rider begins to lift himself from the saddle . . .

The upper body is thrown slightly too much forward.

The equilibrium is now restored and the hand begins to give.

The seat is to come gently down into the saddle. The hand is open and will not close until after the landing.

The rider's upper body returns to the upright position.

The rider's rhythmic, swaying approach with the seat near the saddle assists the horse's activity.

Here the leg goes a little back. The hand is still restraining, but light.

. . . to give the horse the chance to get his hindlegs under as much as possible.

The hand still fixed, the elbows turn outwards.

The horse arches himself correctly because the rider gives him complete freedom and the seat is out of the saddle.

The knee and heel come up simultaneously.

On landing, the legs come forward.

The equilibrium is restored, the leg is in the correct place.

Harvey Smith O'Malley

Wall 1.65 m

The rider sits well down in the saddle — presumably he notices that he is getting too close to the fence.

Still waiting to see. The horse's head is very high, hence the raised hands.

The upper body now goes forward slightly.

The leg is applied, the hand goes back a little.

Gently yielding, the knee nearly straight.

Here the horse is given all the freedom he needs.

The rider's light hand is still stretched.

The yielding is correct.

The horse is now restrained.

The horse is now given more freedom and has an opportunity to get his hindquarters well under.

The line of the take-off has been well chosen, the seat comes up, the hindlegs are well under.

The hand is still restraining.

Here, the horse is free. The rider in perfect balance.

The seat meets the saddle the moment the horse begins to land.

Even on landing the horse gets full freedom.

The bent hindlegs — the result of the rider's yielding.

Upright fence 1.60 m

David Broome   Mr Softee

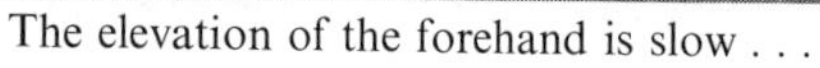

The elevation of the forehand is slow . . .

. . . but is improved by the powerful bending of the hocks . . .

Raimondo d'Inzeo   Bellevue

The hindlegs well under . . .

. . . compensating d'Inzeo's forward-bent body . . .

. . . giving a wide angle of elevation . . .

Alwin Schockemöhle   Donald Rex

An unusual way of shifting the centre of gravity backwards . . .

. . . to facilitate the elevation of the forehand . . .

Schockemöhle has developed a peculiar though effective technique, which the average rider should be careful to avoid. Broome's stiff knee and typical hands can be noticed in the first pictures, but this is corrected later. Note the similar style of Broome and d'Inzeo over this fence. Compare the horses' different jumping techniques. Mr Softee jumps "without using his back", Bellevue with an acceptable back action, Donald Rex with excellent back action.

. . . however, not as good as with Donald Rex.

. . . to reach far at an early take-off. (See the Form of the Take-off.)

. . . and attaining a good elevation. (See the First and Second Parts of the Take-off.)

Upright fence 1.60 m

David Broome Mr Softee

Neck stretched, forelegs bent.

Neck lifted, forelegs stretched. (See Reflexes.)

Raimondo d'Inzeo Bellevue

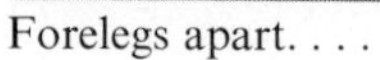

Forelegs apart. . . .

. . . the weight on the off foreleg . . .

Alwin Schockemöhle Donald Rex

The neck bent — the hindlegs bent. (See Reflexes.)

Note the similarity between these three riders and their horses — during the landing. It shows that, when the horse has reached the peak of the leap, there is not much for the rider to do, except to retain his balance in accordance with that of the horse. This is easier to do here than during the approach and the take-off.

. . . is transferred to the near foreleg.

This technique prevents a mistake, as a burdened foreleg cannot bend.

The horse is not balanced but . . .

. . . compensates with a long stride.

Jan-Olof Wannius

Born in 1942. Raised in a family devoted to horses. His father owns Djursholm Riding School, where Jan-Olof started to ride as a nine-year-old. The following year, he entered a competition. At the end of the 'fifties, he entered various national competitions and began his international jumping career in the mid-'sixties. Amongst his greater successes were: third place in the European Championship Grand Prix, Rotterdam 1967; second place in the Irish Trophy in Dublin, 1968; winner of the *Daily Telegraph* Cup, Wembley 1969; and sixth place in the European Championship at Hickstead, 1969. His most successful horses are Shalimar, Shirokko and Goldfinger.

Jan-Olof Wannius Shalimar

Oxer 1.60 × 1.80 m

The horse is full of impulsion.

The rider finds himself too far from the correct take-off line.

Rider and horse are co-ordinated and balanced correctly.

The horse is allowed to raise his head.

The tremendous impulsion causes the rider's upper body to be thrown too much forwards-downwards.

The balance is perfect. The rider begins to straighten the "ugly" elbows. The position of the leg is correct and the leg still active.

Here the rider rises, but has shifted the centre of gravity to the left.

The seat still has no contact with the saddle, and the horse has no difficulty in bending his hindlegs.

The rider is driving hard towards the fence.

To put in an extra stride or continue a bold approach? He chooses the latter.

The rider has his foot back in the stirrup and thus eases his seat, giving the horse a chance to put his hindlegs under him.

There is hardly any give. The elbows go up.

Shalimar doesn't use his back ideally.

The horse has reached well and now begins the landing.

The horse is still completely free.

The rider has full control of the horse and the fast canter continues with a turn to the left.

Oxer 1.60 × 1.80 m

Raimondo d'Inzeo   Bow Jack

In this phase, Bow Jack has his front legs very much bent.

David Broome   Top of the Morning

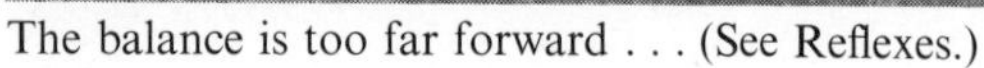

The balance is too far forward . . . (See Reflexes.)

. . . under the horse . . .

Jonqueres d'Oriola   Pomone

The hindlegs stretch . . .

. . . touch the ground . . .

. . . and bend . . .

Here is a large, wide fence. To avoid knocking down the further bar, the take-off must not be too far away (as with a straight up-and-down). This demands, on the other hand, a sudden elevation from the horse which is counteracted by the rider in throwing his upper body forward to establish correct balance. Broome's lack of contact, with reins too long, makes the elbows point outwards which, besides looking ugly, must influence balance and effectiveness.

. . . and increases the elevation.

. . . to again stretch in taking-off. (See Second Part of the Take-off.)

Impulsion is terminated early — explosive power. (See Muscles.)

Oxer 1.60 × 1.80 m

Raimondo d'Inzeo   Bow Jack

Forelegs stretching too soon . . .

. . . indicate that the top of the jumping curve has come early. The take-off too far away?

. . . the landing is relatively close to the fence.

David Broome   Top of the Morning

Forelegs bent late in the jump . . .

. . . indicate that the jumping curve has been reached too late.

The landing is far from the fence.

Jonqueres d'Oriola   Pomone

Even here, the bent forelegs are late in the actual jump.

Powerful knee action.

These sequences show an uncanny similarity between these three top riders. The landing after the wide fence is steeper and demands that the upper part of the rider's body must be in a more upright position.

Abnormal movement in canter to the left.

Alwin Schockemöhle

Born in a German farming family in 1937. Now owner of an iron and steel business. His schooling seems ideal for the Hannoverian breed of horse, and he has successfully ridden a number of horses in international jumping competitions, and has won many during the last ten years. Amongst his most successful horses are: Ferdl, Freiherr and Bacchus. A few years ago he won the record sum of 46,000 DM in nine competitions on Wimpel and Donald Rex. The latter is considered one of the world's best jumping horses of today. Schockemöhle holds the German high jumping record of 2.25m. He won the gold medal at the Rome Olympics in 1960 and successfully took part in the Olympic competitions in Mexico in 1968.

Alwin Schockemöhle   Donald Rex

Upright fence 1.60 m

Not right. The rider sits down in the saddle in an exaggerated manner, but doesn't pull at the reins.

The half-halt is finished, the horse is well collected with the hindlegs well under.

Continued forward movement of the upper body without the head moving.

The upper body moves forward, the seat tends to lift, the arms come forward with the hands on the crest.

Here the horse is given all the freedom he wants. The back can work freely and the neck will stretch.

The arms are stretched forward, the hands are now correct. Reins held with featherlight contact with the horse's mouth.

Straight forelegs just before landing.

The moment the horse lands, the rider is again in full control through gentle restraint.

Full control of the horse, upper body vertical, the hands light and ready.

The upper body on its way forward, the foot shifted back a little, the hands raised, the horse's head and neck elevated.

The rider takes his weight off the horse's back. The hands are exaggeratedly raised towards the chest.

The upper body is thrown forward, thus stretching the knee, the hands begin to move forward.

The seat still off the saddle, the foot slightly back.

The horse prepares for the landing, completely free neck. The seat gently meets the saddle.

Tail in the air. Determined riding towards the next fence.

The distance to the next fence allows a few strides (not many) with a light seat.

Upright fence 1.45 m

Sarah Roger-Smith   Gambit

Near hindfoot touches the ground after off forefoot.

Movement of the feet as in canter to the right.

Jan-Olof Wannius   Goldfinger

Off hindfoot touches ground after off forefoot.

Movement of the feet as in cross canter.

Hartwig Steenken   Porta Westfalica

When the hind feet touch the ground close together . . .

. . . the impulsion of both hindlegs is simultaneous.

This is jumping on time. Compare two relatively inexperienced horses, Gambit and Goldfinger, with the more expert Porta Westfalica; Sarah Roger-Smith is not quite balanced but tries not to disturb the horse. Jan-Olof Wannius has been forced to a severe restraint and helps the horse over the fence. Hartwig Steenken and Porta Westfalica are a well-matched pair. Note the horse's excellent foreleg technique and fantastic parabola.

The impulsion of the hindquarters is still not terminated.

Both hocks are here stretched further than with the other horses.

The impulsion of the hindquarters is noticeably quickly terminated.

Upright fence 1.45 m

Sarah Roger-Smith   Gambit

Forelegs well apart — a safe landing.

Jan-Olof Wannius   Goldfinger

Wide forefoot support reduces the horse's balance problems.

Hartwig Steenken   Porta Westfalica

Late separation of the forelegs . . .
. . . gives too little forefoot support.

Once over the fence all riders turn slightly to the right towards the next fence. Wannius' leg is a bit unsteady, the others keep theirs well in place. Steenken bends his body forward (as he usually does) in the stride after the fence which unnecessarily burdens the horse's forehand. The hands of the riders are light and in perfect positions.

The horse's off hindleg well forward.

Correct canter to the right.

The upper body of the rider is thrown forward on landing. (See First Stride after Landing.)

Cross canter.

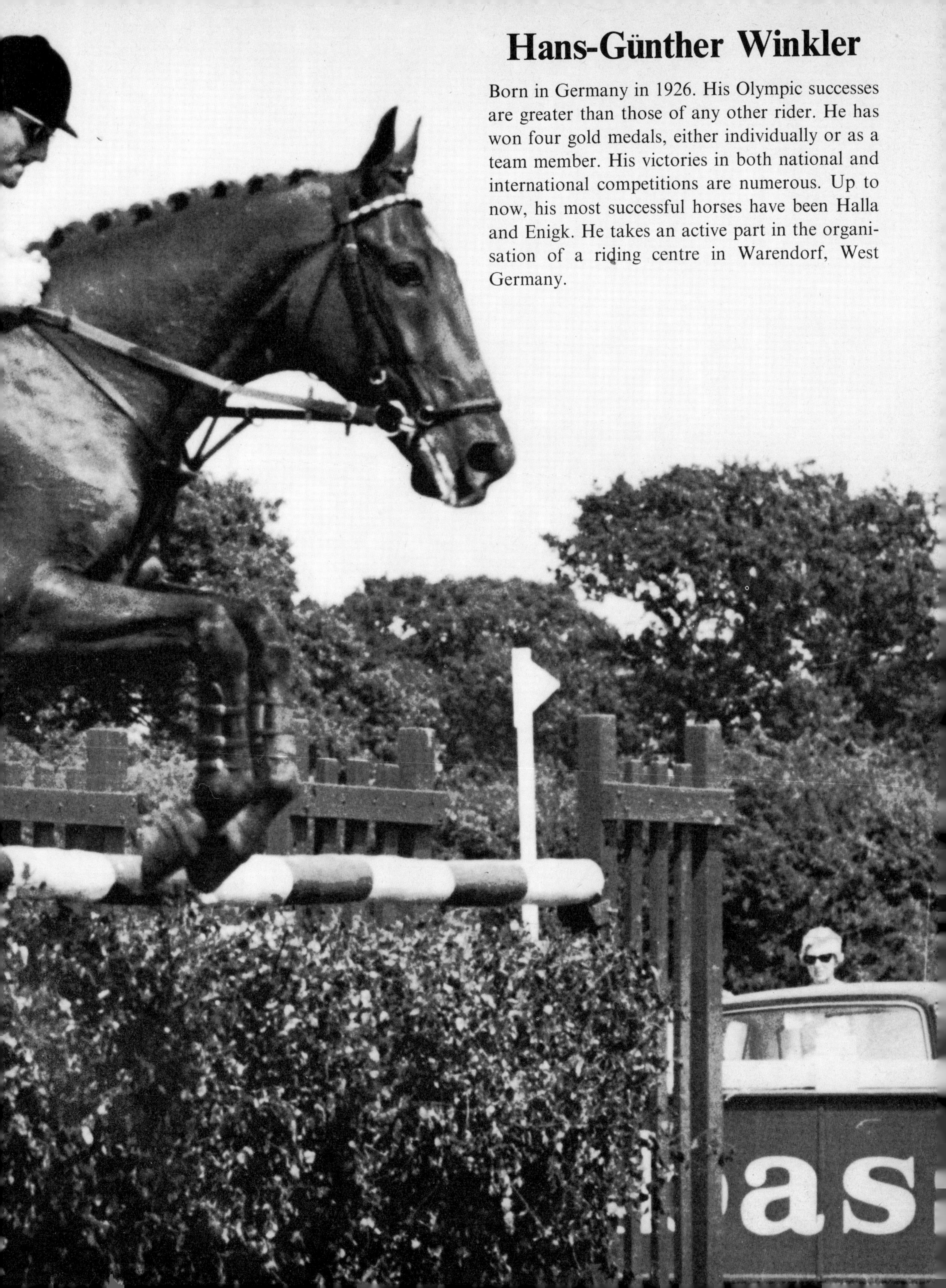

Hans-Günther Winkler

Born in Germany in 1926. His Olympic successes are greater than those of any other rider. He has won four gold medals, either individually or as a team member. His victories in both national and international competitions are numerous. Up to now, his most successful horses have been Halla and Enigk. He takes an active part in the organisation of a riding centre in Warendorf, West Germany.

Hans-Günther Winkler Torphy

Upright fence 1.60 m

Horse and rider balanced and concentrating.

The leg is moved to the girth.

All is ready for a take-off from exactly the right point.

The body slightly forward. The rein yields.

Horse and rider both at the moment of stretching.

The leg remains too far back, but the rider is in perfect balance and the yielding is just right.

Too tense, the back of the rider slackens, the leg moves forward.

The rider already prepares the horse for a turn to the left.

The horse is correct. No noticeable rein action, but no yielding.

The hand is pushed forward a little. Otherwise the rider is in the same position as before, knowing that all is right and correct.

Keeping his balance and easing the seat, the rider makes it easier for the horse to get his hindlegs as far under as possible.

Fully yielding. The horse now has the opportunity of using all his technique.

The rider begins to bend his back a little . . .

. . . which is here clearly noticeable. Thus the seat gets too near the saddle too soon.

The body a little too straight at the moment of landing.

The upper body goes forward a little, the leg also goes backwards. The equilibrium is co-ordinated with that of the horse.

Wall 1.65 m

Hans-Günther Winkler   Enigk

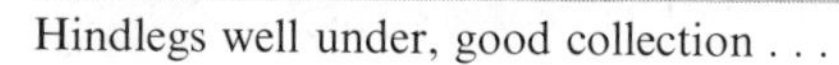
Hindlegs well under, good collection . . .

. . . allowing freedom of the neck . . .

David Broome   Mr Softee

Collection by shifting the centre of gravity — head and neck raised.

Alwin Schockemöhle   Wimpel

Impulsion from the hindlegs at exactly the same point with all three horses. (See the Second Part of the Take-off.)

The difference in styles is due to Broome's shorter martingale. The yielding from all riders is slight but sufficient, so as not to disturb the horses. Note that the toe of all the riders points downwards and regains normal position just above the fence.

. . . and good elevation is attained.

The angle of the head remains in the same position during the complete jump.

The angle of the head is gradually altered during the jump.

The Authors

INGVAR FREDRICSON

A veterinary surgeon and university lecturer in anatomy and histology at the Royal Veterinary High School in Sweden. In co-operation with the Veterinary High School, Saab-Scania and F.O.A. he is leading a research project regarding the cinematics and co-ordination of active joint movements. He is the author of Sections One and Two and of the picture series.

ANDERS GERNANDT

A former Cavalry Supply Corps officer, he was an instructor in jumping at the Strömsholm Riding School from 1952—3. In 1964 he was engaged as manager by Swedish Radio. He has taken part in both dressage and jumping competitions and participated in the Olympic Games in Stockholm, 1956 and 1960. He is a TV commentator for equine sports. He is the author of the comments on the picture series.

GUNNAR HEDLUND

Master of Skånsta Riding School, he has passed RIK I at Strömsholm, and was the author of the bestseller *Handbok for Ryttare* (Beckmans). He trained as an artist in Paris and has executed all the line drawings in *Horses and Jumping*.

LARS SEDERHOLM

He received his basic riding education in dressage with Henri St Cyr, the successful Swedish Olympic rider. Since 1958 he has been active in England, becoming English champion in cross-country competitions in 1963, '64 and '65. He owns the Waterstock House Training Centre, near Oxford, and is considered one of the leading English trainers in cross-country riding and show jumping. He is the author of the section 'Training and Riding Jumping Horses'.